Holt Algebra 1

Know-It Notebook™

HOLT, RINEHART AND WINSTON

A Harcourt Education Company

Orlando • Austin • New York • San Diego • London

Printed in the United States of America

ISBN 978-0-03-077923-7
ISBN 0-03-077923-5

6 7 8 9 862 09

Contents

Using KIN iv
Notetaking Strategies 2
Chapter 1 Key Vocabulary 4
Lesson 1-1 6
Lesson 1-2 7
Lesson 1-3 9
Lesson 1-4 11
Lesson 1-5 12
Lesson 1-6 15
Lesson 1-7 16
Lesson 1-8 18
Chapter 1 Review 20
Chapter 1 Big Idea Questions 23
Chapter 2 Key Vocabulary 24
Lesson 2-1 26
Lesson 2-2 27
Lesson 2-3 29
Lesson 2-4 30
Lesson 2-5 31
Lesson 2-6 32
Lesson 2-7 34
Lesson 2-8 35
Lesson 2-9 37
Lesson 2-10 38
Chapter 2 Review 39
Chapter 2 Big Idea Questions 43
Chapter 3 Key Vocabulary 44
Lesson 3-1 46
Lesson 3-2 47
Lesson 3-3 48
Lesson 3-4 50
Lesson 3-5 51
Lesson 3-6 52
Chapter 3 Review 54
Chapter 3 Big Idea Questions 57
Chapter 4 Key Vocabulary 58
Lesson 4-1 60
Lesson 4-2 61
Lesson 4-3 62
Lesson 4-4 63
Lesson 4-5 64
Lesson 4-6 66
Chapter 4 Review 67
Chapter 4 Big Idea Questions 71
Chapter 5 Key Vocabulary 72
Lesson 5-1 74
Lesson 5-2 75
Lesson 5-3 76
Lesson 5-4 78
Lesson 5-5 79
Lesson 5-6 80
Lesson 5-7 81
Lesson 5-8 82
Lesson 5-9 84
Chapter 5 Review 86
Chapter 5 Big Idea Questions 91
Chapter 6 Key Vocabulary 92
Lesson 6-1 94
Lesson 6-2 95
Lesson 6-3 96
Lesson 6-4 98
Lesson 6-5 100
Lesson 6-6 101
Chapter 6 Review 102
Chapter 6 Big Idea Questions 105
Chapter 7 Key Vocabulary 106
Lesson 7-1 108
Lesson 7-2 109
Lesson 7-3 111
Lesson 7-4 113
Lesson 7-5 115
Lesson 7-6 117
Lesson 7-7 118
Lesson 7-8 119
Chapter 7 Review 120
Chapter 7 Big Idea Questions 123
Chapter 8 Key Vocabulary 124
Lesson 8-1 126
Lesson 8-2 127
Lesson 8-3 128
Lesson 8-4 129
Lesson 8-5 130
Lesson 8-6 131
Chapter 8 Review 132
Chapter 8 Big Idea Questions 135
Chapter 9 Key Vocabulary 136
Lesson 9-1 138
Lesson 9-2 140
Lesson 9-3 143
Lesson 9-4 144
Lesson 9-5 145
Lesson 9-6 146
Lesson 9-7 147
Lesson 9-8 148
Lesson 9-9 150
Chapter 9 Review 152
Chapter 9 Big Idea Questions 157
Chapter 10 Key Vocabulary 158
Lesson 10-1 160
Lesson 10-2 161
Lesson 10-3 162
Lesson 10-4 164
Lesson 10-5 165
Lesson 10-6 167
Lesson 10-7 169
Lesson 10-8 170
Chapter 10 Review 173
Chapter 10 Big Idea Questions 177
Chapter 11 Key Vocabulary 178
Lesson 11-1 180
Lesson 11-2 181
Lesson 11-3 182
Lesson 11-4 184
Lesson 11-5 185
Lesson 11-6 187
Lesson 11-7 189
Lesson 11-8 190
Lesson 11-9 191
Chapter 11 Review 192
Chapter 11 Big Idea Questions 196
Chapter 12 Key Vocabulary 198
Lesson 12-1 200
Lesson 12-2 201
Lesson 12-3 203
Lesson 12-4 204
Lesson 12-5 205
Lesson 12-6 206
Lesson 12-7 207
Chapter 12 Review 208
Chapter 12 Big Idea Questions 211

USING THE *KNOW-IT NOTEBOOK*™

This *Know-It Notebook* will help you take notes, organize your thinking, and study for quizzes and tests. There are *Know-It Notes*™ pages for every lesson in your textbook. These notes will help you identify important mathematical information that you will need later.

Know-It Notes

Vocabulary

One good note-taking practice is to keep a list of the new vocabulary.

- Use the page references or the glossary in your textbook to find each definition and a clarifying example.
- Write each definition and example on the lines provided.

Lesson Objectives

Another good note-taking practice is to know the objective the content covers.

Additional Examples

Your textbook includes examples for each math concept taught. Additional examples in the *Know-It Notebook* help you take notes to remember how to solve different types of problems.

- Take notes as your teacher discusses each example.
- Write notes in the blank boxes to help you remember key concepts.
- Write final answers in the shaded boxes.

Check It Out

Complete the Check It Out problems that follow each lesson. Use these to make sure you understand the math concepts covered in the lesson.

- Write each answer in the space provided.
- Check your answers with your teacher or another student.
- Ask your teacher to help you understand any problem that you answered incorrectly.

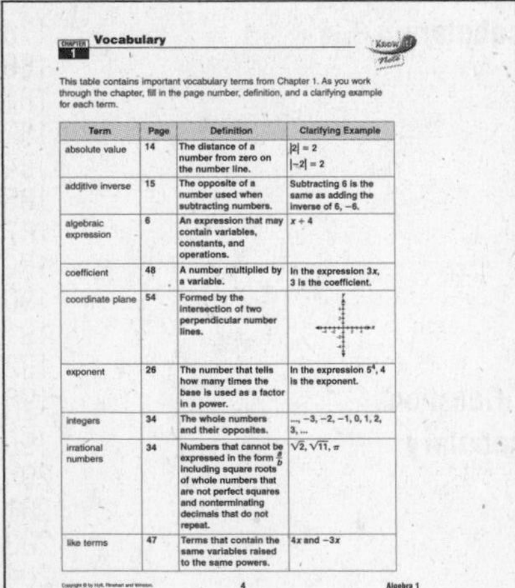

CHAPTER 1 **Vocabulary**

This table contains important vocabulary terms from Chapter 1. As you work through the chapter, fill in the page number, definition, and a clarifying example for each term.

Term	Page	Definition	Clarifying Example
absolute value	14	The distance of a number from zero on the number line.	$\|2\| = 2$ $\|-2\| = 2$
additive inverse	15	The opposite of a number used when subtracting numbers.	Subtracting 6 is the same as adding the inverse of 6, −6.
algebraic expression	6	An expression that may contain variables, constants, and operations.	$x + 4$
coefficient	48	A number multiplied by a variable.	In the expression $3x$, 3 is the coefficient.
coordinate plane	54	Formed by the intersection of two perpendicular number lines.	
exponent	26	The number that tells how many times the base is used as a factor in a power.	In the expression 5^4, 4 is the exponent.
integers	34	The whole numbers and their opposites.	…, −3, −2, −1, 0, 1, 2, 3, …
irrational numbers	34	Numbers that cannot be expressed in the form $\frac{a}{b}$ including square roots of whole numbers that are not perfect squares and nonterminating decimals that do not repeat.	$\sqrt{2}, \sqrt{11}, \pi$
like terms	47	Terms that contain the same variables raised to the same powers.	$4x$ and $-3x$

Copyright © by Holt, Rinehart and Winston. All rights reserved. 4 Algebra 1

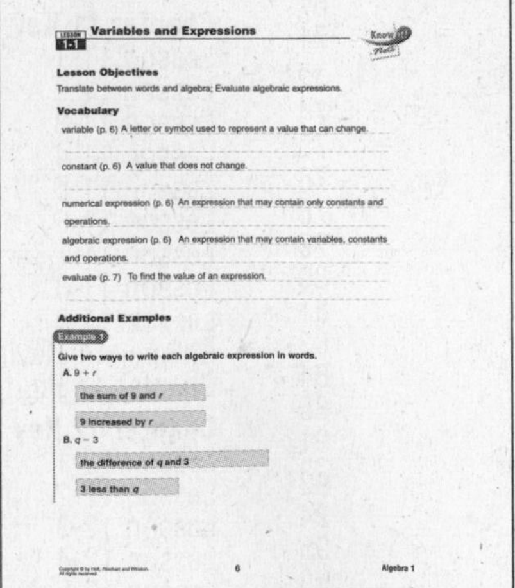

LESSON 1-1 **Variables and Expressions**

Lesson Objectives

Translate between words and algebra; Evaluate algebraic expressions.

Vocabulary

variable (p. 6) A letter or symbol used to represent a value that can change.

constant (p. 6) A value that does not change.

numerical expression (p. 6) An expression that may contain only constants and operations.

algebraic expression (p. 6) An expression that may contain variables, constants and operations.

evaluate (p. 7) To find the value of an expression.

Additional Examples

Example 1

Give two ways to write each algebraic expression in words.

A. $9 + r$

the sum of 9 and r

9 increased by r

B. $q - 3$

the difference of q and 3

3 less than q

Copyright © by Holt, Rinehart and Winston. All rights reserved. 6 Algebra 1

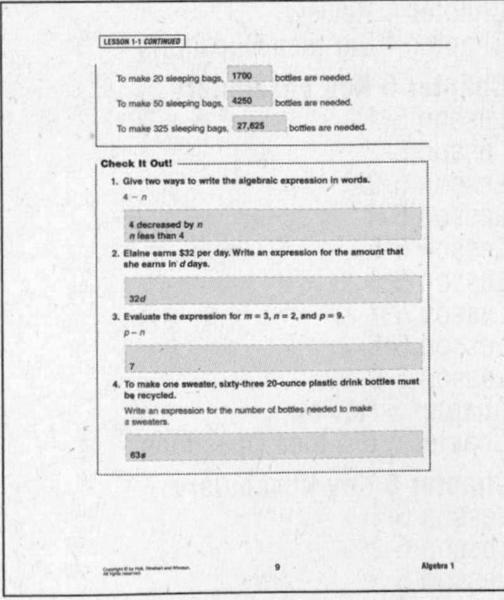

LESSON 1-1 *CONTINUED*

To make 20 sleeping bags, 1700 bottles are needed.

To make 50 sleeping bags, 4250 bottles are needed.

To make 325 sleeping bags, 27,625 bottles are needed.

Check It Out!

1. Give two ways to write the algebraic expression in words.

   $4 - n$

   4 decreased by n
   n less than 4

2. Elaine earns $32 per day. Write an expression for the amount that she earns in d days.

   $32d$

3. Evaluate the expression for $m = 3$, $n = 2$, and $p = 9$.

   $p - n$

   7

4. To make one sweater, sixty-three 20-ounce plastic drink bottles must be recycled.

   Write an expression for the number of bottles needed to make s sweaters.

   $63s$

Copyright © by Holt, Rinehart and Winston. All rights reserved. 9 Algebra 1

Key Concepts

Key concepts from each lesson are included. These are indicated in your student book with the KIN logo.

- Write each answer in the space provided.
- Check your answers with your book.
- Ask your teacher to help you with any concept that you don't understand.

Chapter Review

Complete Chapter Review problems that follow each lesson. This is a good review before you take the chapter test.

- Write each answer in the space provided.
- Check your answers with your teacher or another student.
- Ask your teacher to help you understand any problem that you answered incorrectly.

Big Ideas

The Big Ideas have you summarize the important chapter concepts in your own words. Putting ideas in your words requires that you think about the ideas and understand them. This will also help you remember them.

- Write each answer in the space provided.
- Check your answers with your teacher or another student.
- Ask your teacher to help you understand any question that you answered incorrectly.

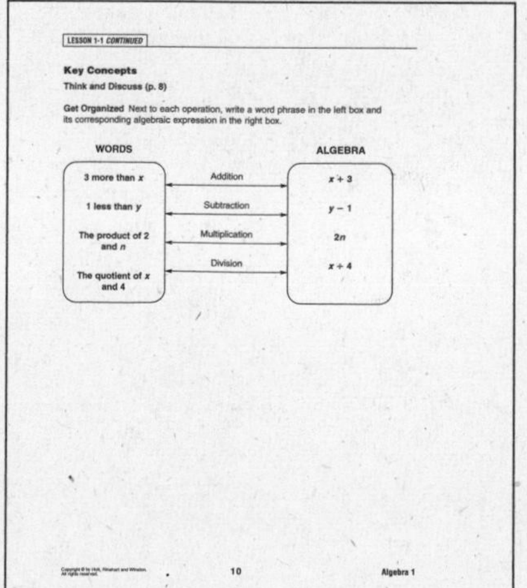

LESSON 1-1 *CONTINUED*

Key Concepts

Think and Discuss (p. 8)

Get Organized Next to each operation, write a word phrase in the left box and its corresponding algebraic expression in the right box.

WORDS		ALGEBRA
3 more than x	Addition	$x + 3$
1 less than y	Subtraction	$y - 1$
The product of 2 and n	Multiplication	$2n$
The quotient of x and 4	Division	$x \div 4$

Copyright © by Holt, Rinehart and Winston. All rights reserved. 10 Algebra 1

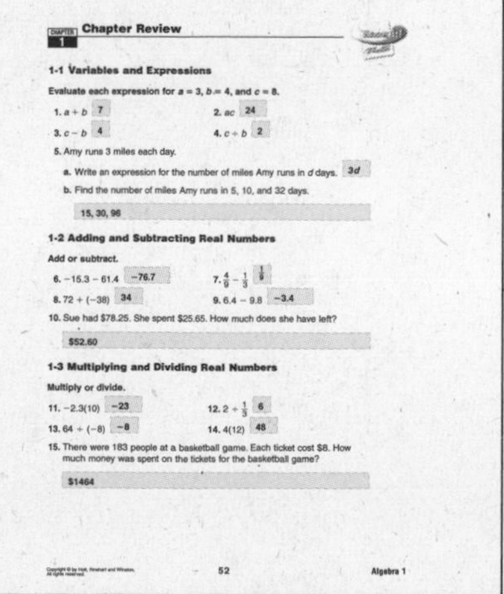

CHAPTER 1 **Chapter Review**

1-1 Variables and Expressions

Evaluate each expression for $a = 3$, $b = 4$, and $c = 8$.

1. $a + b$ **7**
2. ac **24**
3. $c - b$ **4**
4. $c \div b$ **2**
5. Amy runs 3 miles each day.
   a. Write an expression for the number of miles Amy runs in d days. **$3d$**
   b. Find the number of miles Amy runs in 5, 10, and 32 days. **15, 30, 96**

1-2 Adding and Subtracting Real Numbers

Add or subtract.

6. $-15.3 - 61.4$ **-76.7**
7. $\frac{4}{9} - \frac{1}{3}$ **$\frac{1}{9}$**
8. $72 + (-38)$ **34**
9. $6.4 - 9.8$ **-3.4**
10. Sue had $78.25. She spent $25.65. How much does she have left? **$52.60**

1-3 Multiplying and Dividing Real Numbers

Multiply or divide.

11. $-2.3(10)$ **-23**
12. $2 \div \frac{1}{3}$ **6**
13. $64 \div (-8)$ **-8**
14. $4(12)$ **48**
15. There were 183 people at a basketball game. Each ticket cost $8. How much money was spent on the tickets for the basketball game? **$1464**

Copyright © by Holt, Rinehart and Winston. All rights reserved. 52 Algebra 1

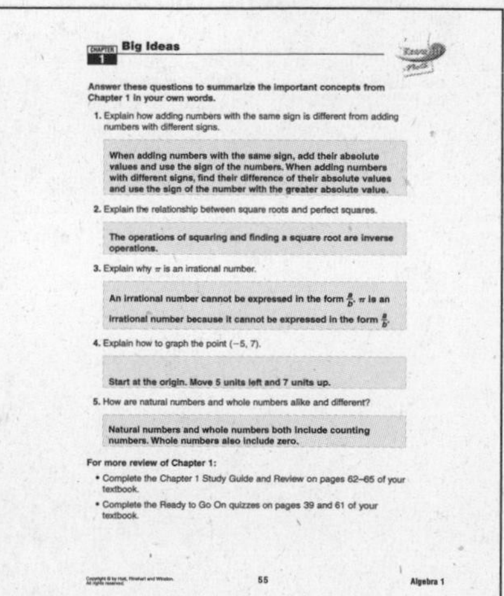

CHAPTER 1 **Big Ideas**

Answer these questions to summarize the important concepts from Chapter 1 in your own words.

1. Explain how adding numbers with the same sign is different from adding numbers with different signs.
   When adding numbers with the same sign, add their absolute values and use the sign of the numbers. When adding numbers with different signs, find their difference of their absolute values and use the sign of the number with the greater absolute value.
2. Explain the relationship between square roots and perfect squares.
   The operations of squaring and finding a square root are inverse operations.
3. Explain why π is an irrational number.
   An irrational number cannot be expressed in the form $\frac{a}{b}$. π is an irrational number because it cannot be expressed in the form $\frac{a}{b}$.
4. Explain how to graph the point $(-5, 7)$.
   Start at the origin. Move 5 units left and 7 units up.
5. How are natural numbers and whole numbers alike and different?
   Natural numbers and whole numbers both include counting numbers. Whole numbers also include zero.

For more review of Chapter 1:

- Complete the Chapter 1 Study Guide and Review on pages 62–65 of your textbook.
- Complete the Ready to Go On quizzes on pages 39 and 61 of your textbook.

Copyright © by Holt, Rinehart and Winston. All rights reserved. 55 Algebra 1

NOTE TAKING STRATEGIES

Taking good notes is very important in many of your classes and will be even more important when you take college classes. This Notebook was designed to help you get started. Here are some other steps that can help you take good notes.

Getting Ready

1. Use a loose-leaf notebook. You can add pages to this as where and when you want to. It will help keep you organized.

During the Lecture

2. If you are taking notes during a lecture, write the big ideas. Use abbreviations to save time. Do not worry about spelling or writing every word. Use headings to show changes in the topics discussed. Use numbering or bullets to organize supporting ideas under each topic heading. Leave space before each new heading so that you can fill in more information later.

After the Lecture

3. As soon as possible after the lecture, read through your notes and add any information you can so that when you review your notes later, they make sense. You should also summarize the information into key words or key phrases. This will help your comprehension and will help you process the information. These key words and key phrases will be your memory cues when you are reviewing or taking a test. At this time you may also want to write questions to help clarify the meaning of the ideas and facts.
4. Read your notes out loud. As you do this, state the ideas in your own words and do as much as you can by memory. This will help you remember and will also help with your thinking process. It helps you think about and understand the information.
5. Reflect upon the information you have learned. Ask yourself how new information relates to information you already know. Ask how this relates to your personal experience. Ask how you can apply this information and why it is important.

Before the Test

6. Review your notes. Don't wait until the night before the test to do this review. Do frequent reviews. Don't just read through your notes. Put the information in your notes into your own words. If you do this you will be able to connect the new material with material you already know. You will be better prepared for tests. You will have less test anxiety and will have better recall.
7. Summarize your notes. This should be in your own words and should only include the main points that you need to remember. This will help you internalize the information.

Vocabulary

This table contains important vocabulary terms from Chapter 1. As you work through the chapter, fill in the page number, definition, and a clarifying example for each term.

Term	Page	Definition	Clarifying Example
absolute value			
additive inverse			
algebraic expression			
coefficient			
coordinate plane			
exponent			
integers			
irrational numbers			
like terms			

Term	Page	Definition	Clarifying Example
multiplicative inverse			
natural numbers			
numerical expression			
ordered pair			
rational numbers			
real numbers			
reciprocal			
whole numbers			
x-coordinate			
y-coordinate			

Variables and Expressions

Lesson Objectives

Translate between words and algebra; Evaluate algebraic expressions.

Vocabulary

variable (p. 6) ______________________________

____

constant (p. 6) ______________________________

____

numerical expression (p. 6) ______________________________

____

algebraic expression (p. 6) ______________________________

____

evaluate (p. 7) ______________________________

____

Key Concepts

Think and Discuss (p. 8)

Get Organized Next to each operation, write a word phrase in the left box and its corresponding algebraic expression in the right box.

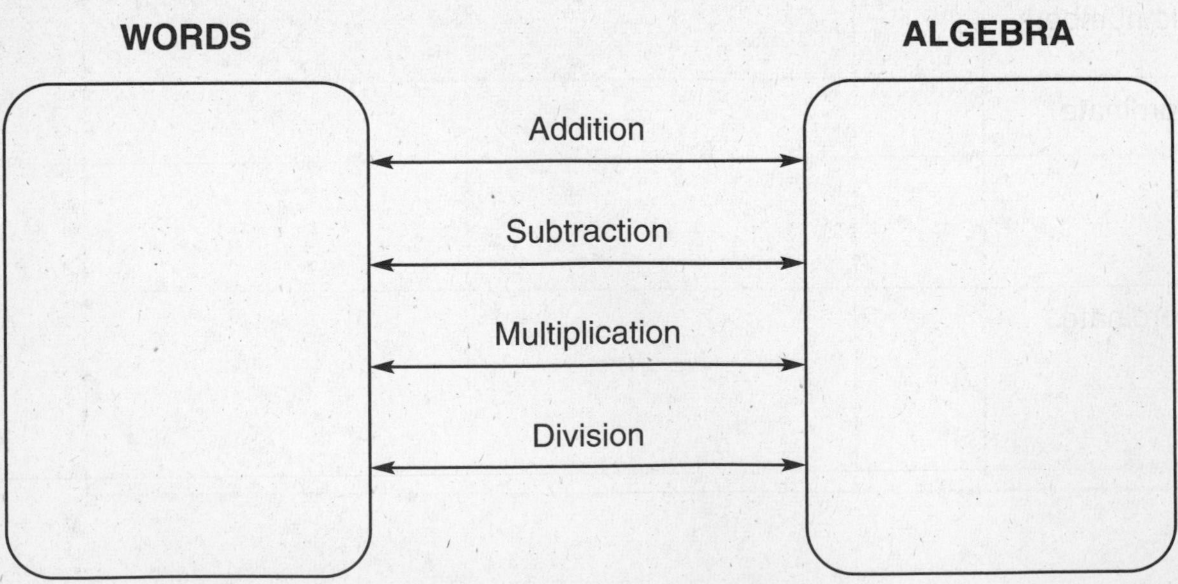

LESSON **1-2**

Adding and Subtracting Real Numbers

Lesson Objectives

Add real numbers; Subtract real numbers

Vocabulary

absolute value (p. 14) ______________________________

____

opposites (p. 15) ______________________________

____

additive inverse (p. 15) ______________________________

____

Key Concepts

Adding Real Numbers (p. 15):

WORDS	NUMBERS
Adding Numbers with the Same Sign	
Adding Numbers with Different Signs	

Subtracting Real Numbers (p. 15):

WORDS	NUMBERS	ALGEBRA

Think and Discuss (p. 17)

Get Organized For each pair of points, tell whether the sum and the difference of the first point and the second point are positive or negative.

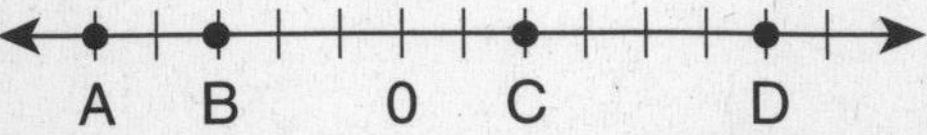

POINTS	SUM	DIFFERENCE
A, B		
B, A		
C, B		
D, A		

LESSON **1-3**

Multiplying and Dividing Real Numbers

Lesson Objectives

Multiply real numbers; Divide real numbers

Vocabulary

reciprocal (p. 21) ______________________________

____

multiplicative inverse (p. 21) ______________________________

____

Key Concepts

Multiplying and Dividing Signed Numbers (p. 21):

WORDS	NUMBERS
Multiplying and Dividing Numbers with the Same Sign	
Multiplying and Dividing Number with Different Signs	

Properties of Zero (p. 21):

WORDS	NUMBERS	ALGEBRA
Multiplication by Zero		
Zero Divided by a Number		
Division by Zero		

Think and Discuss (p. 22)

Get Organized In each blank, write "pos" or "neg" to indicate positive or negative.

Multiplying and Dividing Numbers

MULTIPLICATION	DIVISION
pos × ___ = pos	pos ÷ ___ = pos
pos × ___ = neg	pos ÷ ___ = neg
neg × ___ = neg	neg ÷ ___ = neg
neg × ___ = pos	neg ÷ ___ = pos

Powers and Exponents

Lesson Objectives

Evalute expressions containing exponents

Vocabulary

power (p. 26) ______________________________

____

base (p. 26) ______________________________

____

exponent (p. 26) ______________________________

____

Key Concepts

Think and Discuss (p. 28)

Get Organized In each box, give an example and tell whether the expression is positive or negative.

	Even Exponent	Odd Exponent
Positive Base		
Negative Base		

LESSON 1-5

Square Roots and Real Numbers

Lesson Objectives

Evaluate expressions containing square roots; Classify numbers within the real number system

Vocabulary

square root (p. 32) ____________________

perfect square (p. 32) ____________________

real numbers (p. 34) ____________________

natural numbers (p. 34) ____________________

whole numbers (p. 34) ____________________

integers (p. 34) ____________________

rational numbers (p. 34) ____________________

terminating decimal (p. 34) ____________________

repeating decimal (p. 34) ____________________

irrational numbers (p. 34) ____________________

Key Concepts

Real Numbers (p. 34):

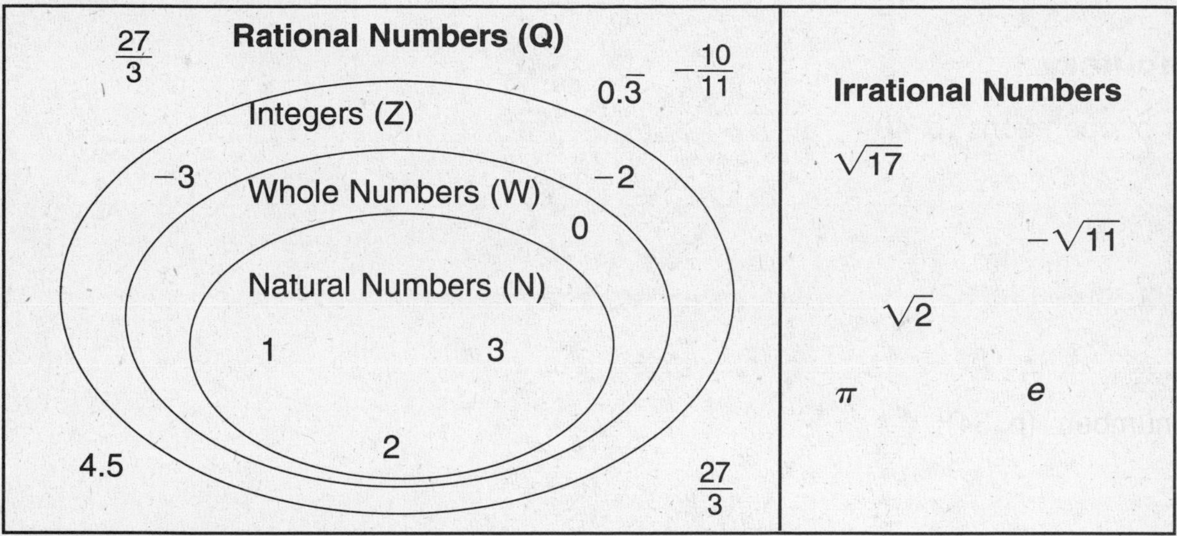

Think and Discuss (p. 35)

Get Organized Use the flowchart to classify each of the given numbers. Write each number in the box with the most specific classification that applies. 4, $\sqrt{25}$, 0, $\frac{1}{3}$, -15, -2.25, $\frac{1}{4}$, $\sqrt{21}$, 2^4, $(-1)^2$

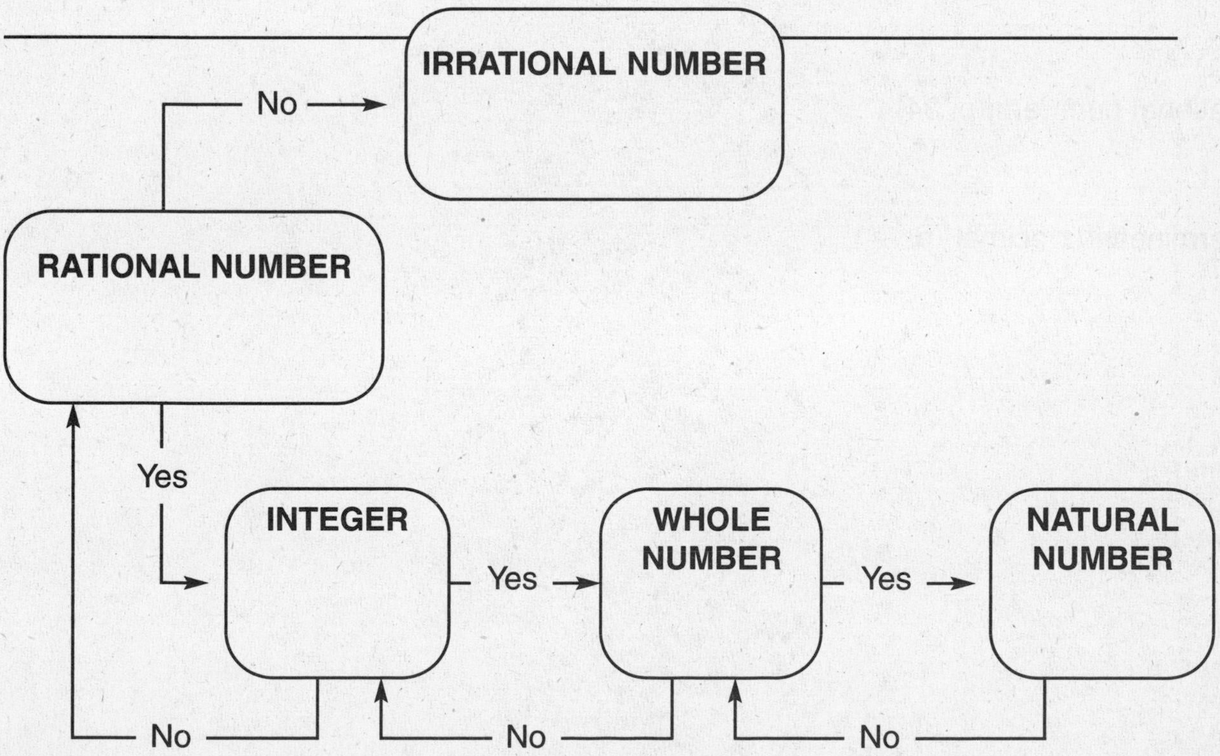

LESSON **1-6**

Order of Operations

Lesson Objectives

Use the order of operations to simplify expressions

Vocabulary

order of operations (p. 40) ______________________________

____

Key Concepts

Order of Operation (p. 40):

Order of Operations	
First:	
Second:	
Third:	
Fourth:	

Think and Discuss (p. 42)

Get Organized In each box, show how grouping symbols can be placed so that the expression is equal to the number shown.

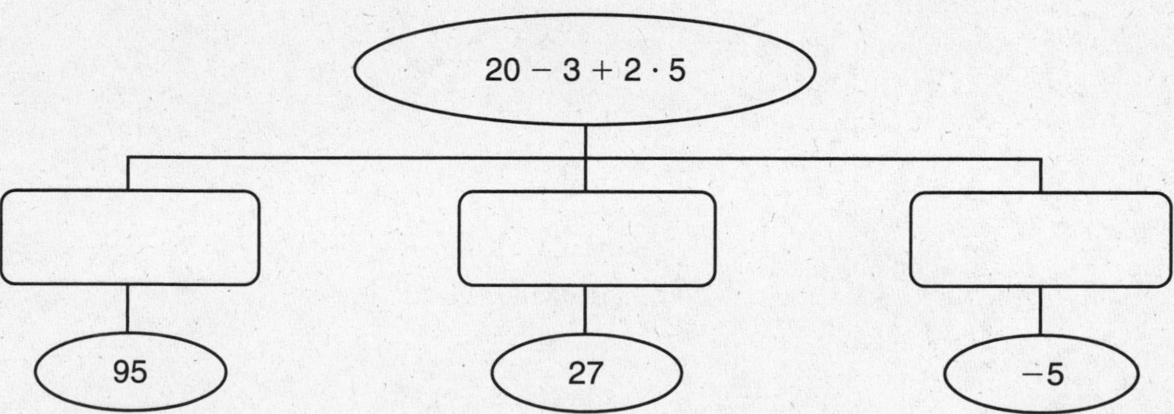

LESSON 1-7

Combining Like Terms

Lesson Objectives

Use the Commutative, Associative, and Distributive Properties to simplify expressions; Combine like terms

Vocabulary

term (p. 47) ______________________________

like terms (p. 47) ______________________________

coefficient (p. 48) ______________________________

Key Concepts

Properties of Addition and Multiplication (p. 46):

WORDS	NUMBERS	ALGEBRA
Commutative Property		
Associative Property		

Distributive Property (p. 47):

WORDS	NUMBERS	ALGEBRA

Think and Discuss (p. 49)

Get Organized In each box, give an example to illustrate the given property.

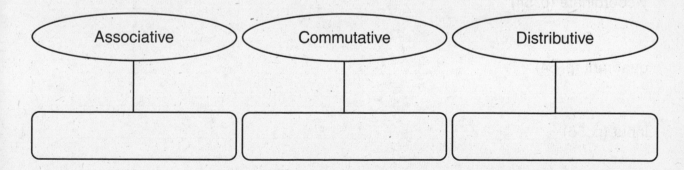

Associative	Commutative	Distributive

Introduction to Functions

Lesson Objectives

Graph ordered pairs in the coordinate plane; Graph functions from ordered pairs

Vocabulary

coordinate plane (p. 54) ______________________________

axes (p. 54) ______________________________

origin (p. 54) ______________________________

x-axis (p. 54) ______________________________

y-axis (p. 54) ______________________________

ordered pair (p. 54) ______________________________

x-coordinate (p. 54) ______________________________

y-coordinate (p. 54) ______________________________

quadrant (p. 54) ______________________________

input (p. 55) ______________________________

output (p. 55) ______________________________

Key Concepts

Think and Discuss (p. 56)

Get Organized In each blank, write "positive" or "negative."

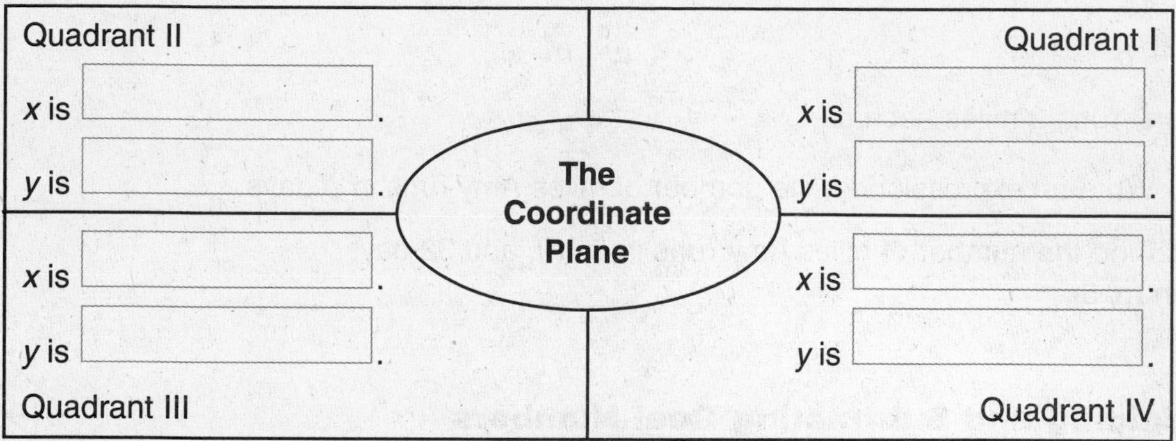

Chapter Review

Know it! Note

1-1 Variables and Expressions

Evaluate each expression for $a = 3$, $b = 4$, and $c = 8$.

1. $a + b$

2. ac

3. $c - b$

4. $c \div b$

5. Amy runs 3 miles each day.

a. Write an expression for the number of miles Amy runs in d days.

b. Find the number of miles Amy runs in 5, 10, and 32 days.

1-2 Adding and Subtracting Real Numbers

Add or subtract.

6. $-15.3 - 61.4$

7. $\frac{4}{9} - \frac{1}{3}$

8. $72 + (-38)$

9. $6.4 - 9.8$

10. Sue had \$78.25. She spent \$25.65. How much does she have left?

1-3 Multiplying and Dividing Real Numbers

Multiply or divide.

11. $-2.3(10)$

12. $2 \div \frac{1}{3}$

13. $64 \div (-8)$

14. $4(12)$

15. There were 183 people at a basketball game. Each ticket cost \$8. How much money was spent on the tickets for the basketball game?

1-4 Powers and Exponents

Write each number as a power of the given base.

16. 16; base −2

17. 1024; base 4

18. 625; base 5

19. −27; base −3

20. A certain species started with two and doubled every day. How many species were there after 8 days?

1-5 Square Roots and Real Numbers

Compare. Write <, >, or =.

21. $\sqrt{121}$ ☐ 10

22. 11 ☐ $\sqrt{144}$

23. 9 ☐ $\sqrt{100}$

24. 6 ☐ $\sqrt{36}$

25. Brian's square pool has an area of 124 ft^2. Estimate the side length of his pool.

1-6 Order of Operations

Evaluate each expression for the given value of *x*.

26. $-x + 5(4)$ for $x = 6$

27. $x^2(9 + 2)$ for $x = 3$

28. $4x \div 2(7) - 1$ for $x = 14$

29. $5(-x^2 - 8)$ for $x = 2$

30. A basketball player's total points can be found by using the expression $1f + 2j + 3t$. Diana made 85 foul shots (f), 106 jump shots (j), and 39 three pointers (t) last season. How many points did she score?

1-7 Simplifying Expressions

Simplify each expression by combining like terms.

31. $8x - 2 + 4x$

32. $-12p + 15p$

33. $6(5 - y) + 5y$

34. $a - 5(2a + a^2)$

Write each product using the Distributive Property. Then simplify.

35. 5(47)

36. 12(104)

37. 11(97)

38. 7(83)

1-8 Introduction to Functions

Generate ordered pairs for each function using the given values for *x*.

39. $y = -3x^2 - 2$; $x = -1, 0, 2$

40. $y = 8 - 2x$; $x = -1, 0, 1$

41. The initial cost of renting a car is \$50 plus 0.25 per mile at Rent-A-Car. Write a rule for the cost of renting a car from Rent-A-Car. Write ordered pairs for the cost of renting a car and driving 50, 100, and 150 miles.

Big Ideas

Answer these questions to summarize the important concepts from Chapter 1 in your own words.

1. Explain how adding numbers with the same sign is different from adding numbers with different signs.

2. Explain the relationship between square roots and perfect squares.

3. Explain why π is an irrational number.

4. Explain how to graph the point $(-5, 7)$.

5. How are natural numbers and whole numbers alike and different?

For more review of Chapter 1:

- Complete the Chapter 1 Study Guide and Review on pages 62–65 of your textbook.
- Complete the Ready to Go On quizzes on pages 39 and 61 of your textbook.

Vocabulary

The table contains important vocabulary terms from Chapter 2. As you work through the chapter, fill in the page number, definition, and a clarifying example.

Term	Page	Definition	Clarifying Example
commission			
contradiction			
conversion factor			
corresponding angles			
corresponding sides			
cross product			
discount			
equation			
formula			
indirect measurement			

Term	Page	Definition	Clarifying Example
markup			
percent			
percent change			
percent decrease			
percent increase			
principle			
proportion			
rate			
ratio			
sales tax			
scale			
scale drawing (model)			
scale factor			
similar			

LESSON 2-1

Solving Equations by Adding or Subtracting

Lesson Objectives

Solve one-step equations in one variable by using addition or subtraction

Vocabulary

equation (p. 77) ______________________________

____

solution of an equation (p. 77) ______________________________

____

Key Concepts

Properties of Equality (p. 79):

WORDS	NUMBERS	ALGEBRA
Addition Property of Equality		
Subtraction Property of Equality		

Think and Discuss (p. 79)

Get Organized In each box, write an example of an equation that can be solved by using the given property, and solve it.

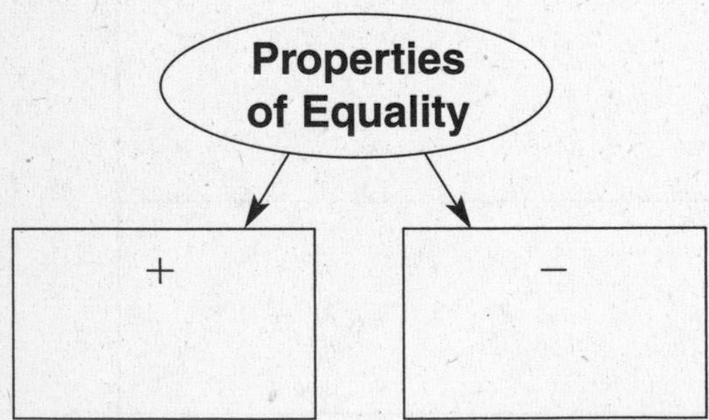

| LESSON 2-2 |

Solving Equations by Multiplying or Dividing

Lesson Objectives

Solve one-step equations in one variable by using multiplication or division

Key Concepts

Property of Equality (p. 86):

WORDS	NUMBERS	ALGEBRA
Addition Property of Equality		
Subtraction Property of Equality		
Multiplication Property of Equality		
Division Property of Equality		

Think and Discuss (p. 87)

Get Organized In each box, write an example of an equation that can be solved by using the given property, and solve it.

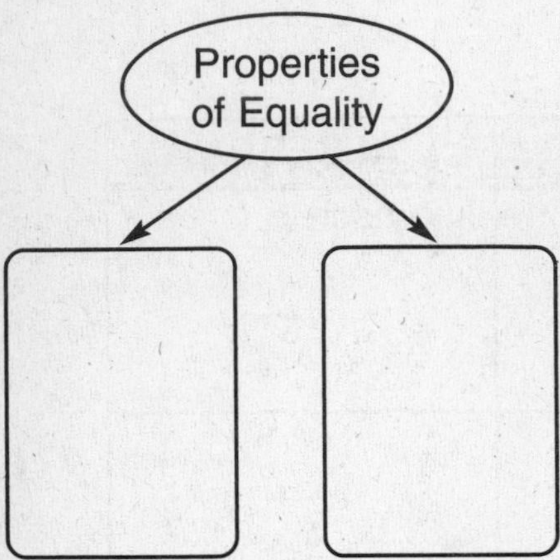

LESSON 2-3

Solving Two-Step and Multi-Step Equations

Lesson Objectives

Solve equations in one variable that contain more than one operation

Key Concepts

Think and Discuss (p. 95)

Get Organized In each box, write and solve a multi-step equation. Use addition, subtraction, multiplication, and division at least one time each.

Solving Multi-Step Equations	

LESSON **2-4**

Solving Equation with Variables on Both Sides

Lesson Objectives

Solve equations in one variable that contain variable terms on both sides

Vocabulary

identity (p. 101): ____________________

____

contradiction (p. 101): ____________________

____

Key Concepts

Identities and Contradictions (p. 101):

WORDS	NUMBERS	ALGEBRA
Identity		
Contradiction		

Think and Discuss (p. 103)

Get Organized In each box, write an equation that has the indicated number of solutions.

An equation with variables on both sides can have. . .

Solving for a Variable

Lesson Objectives

Solve a formula for a given variable; Solve an equation in two or more variables for one of the variables

Vocabulary

formula (p. 107): ______________________________

____

literal equation (p. 108): ______________________________

____

Key Concepts

Solving for a Variable (p. 107):

Solving for a Variable	
Step 1	
Step 2	
Step 3	

Think and Discuss (p. 109)

Get Organized Write a formula that is used in each subject. Then solve the formula for each of its variables.

Common Formulas	
Subject	**Formula**
Geometry	
Physical science	
Earth science	

LESSON **2-6**

Rates, Ratios, and Proportions

Lesson Objectives

Write and use ratios, rates, and unit rates; Write and solve proportions

Vocabulary

ratio (p. 114): ______________________________

____

rate (p. 114): ______________________________

____

scale (p. 116): ______________________________

____

unit rate (p. 114): ______________________________

____

conversion factor (p. 115): ______________________________

____

proportion (p. 114): ______________________________

____

cross products (p. 115): ______________________________

____

scale drawing (p. 116): ______________________________

____

scale model (p. 116): ______________________________

____

Key Concepts

Cross Products property (p. 115):

WORDS	NUMBERS	ALGEBRA
In a proportion, cross products are equal.	$\frac{2}{3} = \frac{4}{6}$ $2 \cdot 6 = 3 \cdot 4$	If $\frac{a}{b} = \frac{c}{d}$ and $b \neq 0$ and $d \neq 0$, then $ad = bc$.

Think and Discuss (p. 117)

Get Organized In each box, write an example of each use of ratios.

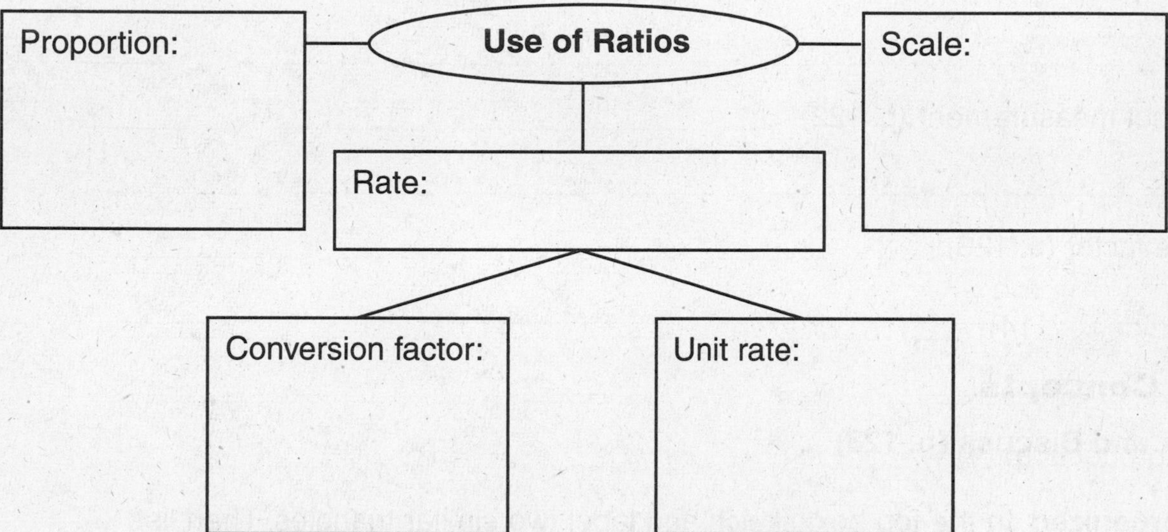

Applications of Proportions

Lesson Objectives

Use proportions to solve problems involving geometric figures; Use proportions and similar figures to measure objects indirectly

Vocabulary

similar (p. 121): ______________________________

corresponding sides (p. 121): ______________________________

corresponding angles (p. 121): ______________________________

indirect measurement (p. 122): ______________________________

scale factor (p. 123): ______________________________

Key Concepts

Think and Discuss (p. 123)

Get organized In the top box, sketch and label two similar triangles. Then list the corresponding sides and angles in the bottom boxes.

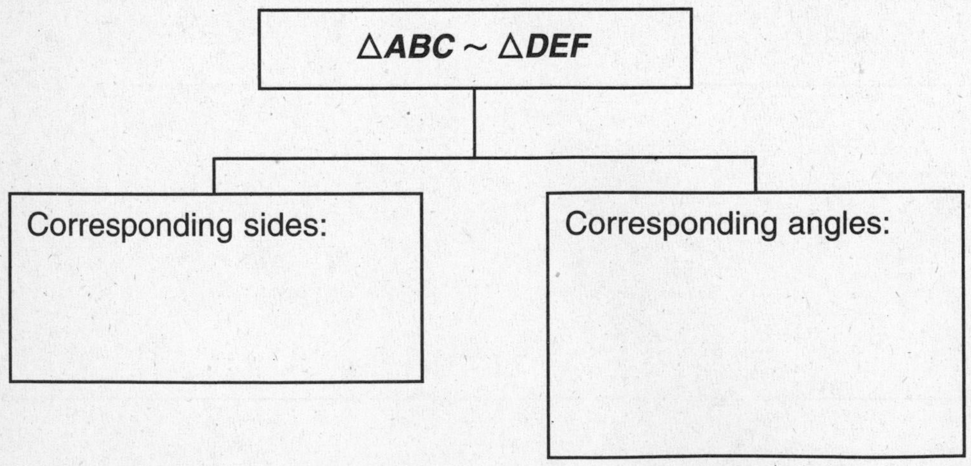

LESSON 2-8 Percents

Lesson Objectives

Solve problems involving percents

Vocabulary

percent (p. 127): ______________________________

____

Key Concepts

Some Common Equivalents (p. 127):

Some Common Equivalents											
Percent	10%	20%	25%	$33\frac{1}{3}\%$	40%	50%	60%	$66\frac{2}{3}\%$	75%	80%	100%
Fraction	$\frac{1}{10}$	$\frac{1}{5}$	$\frac{1}{4}$	$\frac{1}{3}$	$\frac{2}{5}$	$\frac{1}{2}$	$\frac{3}{5}$	$\frac{2}{3}$	$\frac{3}{4}$	$\frac{4}{5}$	1
Decimal	0.1	0.2	0.25	$0.\overline{3}$	0.4	0.5	0.6	$0.\overline{6}$	0.75	0.8	1.0

Think and Discuss (p. 129)

Get organized In each box, write and solve an example using the given method.

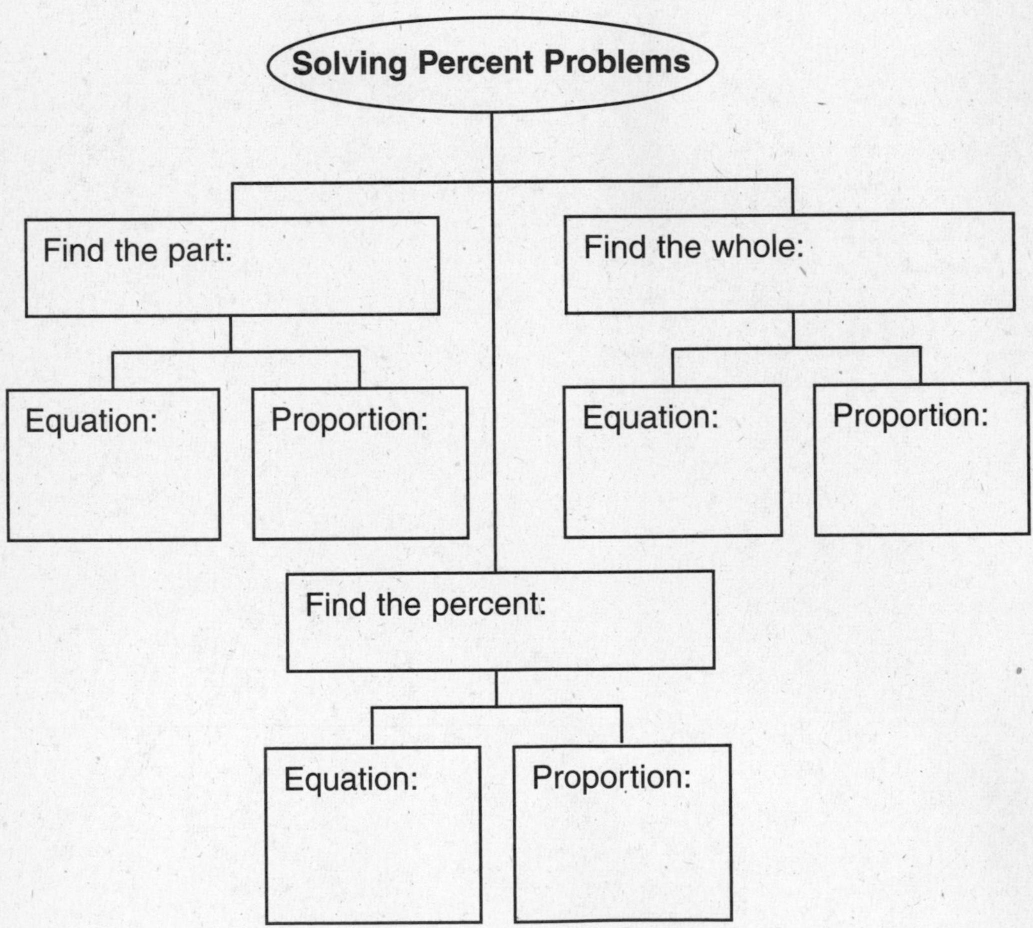

Applications of Percents

Lesson Objectives

Use common applications of percents; Estimate with percents

Vocabulary

commission (p. 133): ______________________________

____

interest (p. 133): ______________________________

____

sales tax (p. 134): ______________________________

____

principal (p. 133): ______________________________

____

tip (p. 134): ______________________________

____

Key Concepts

Think and Discuss (p. 135)

Get organized In each box, write an example of each type of application and find the answer.

Applications of Percents

Commission:	Simple Interest:	Tips:	Sales tax:

LESSON **2-10**

Percent Increase and Decrease

Lesson Objectives

Find percent increase and decrease

Vocabulary

percent change (p. 138): ______________________________

____

percent increase (p. 138): ______________________________

____

percent decrease (p. 138): ______________________________

____

discount (p. 139): ______________________________

____

markup (p. 139): ______________________________

____

Key Concepts

Percent Change (p. 138):

Percent Change
Percent change $= \dfrac{\text{amount of increase or decrease}}{\text{original amount}}$, expressed as a percent

Think and Discuss (p. 140)

Get Organized In each box, write and solve an example of the given type of problem.

Percent Increase	Percent Decrease	Discount	Markup

CHAPTER 2

Chapter Review

2-1 Solving Equations by Adding or Subtracting

Solve each equation.

1. $a + 45 = 36$ 2. $5 - b = 0.65$ 3. $c - \frac{1}{2} = \frac{5}{4}$ 4. $-4.1 + d = -9.8$

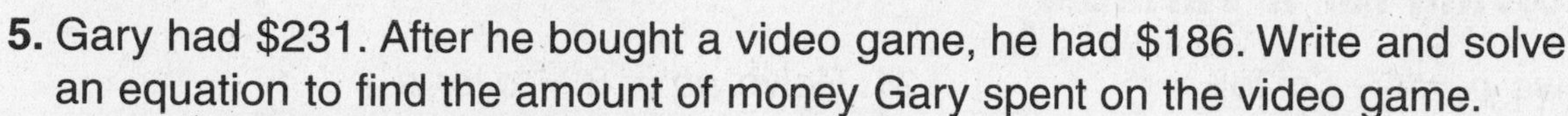

5. Gary had \$231. After he bought a video game, he had \$186. Write and solve an equation to find the amount of money Gary spent on the video game.

2-2 Solving Equations by Multiplying or Dividing

Solve each equation.

6. $5a = 25$ 7. $0.25b = -0.75$ 8. $-\frac{1}{3}c = -\frac{2}{3}$ 9. $-16 = 64d$

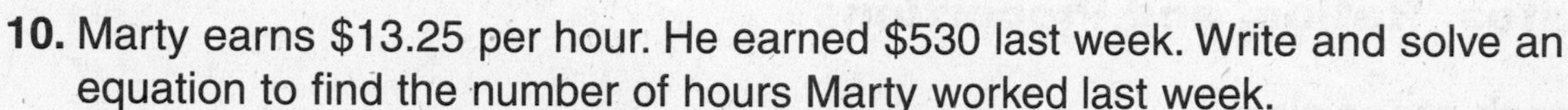

10. Marty earns \$13.25 per hour. He earned \$530 last week. Write and solve an equation to find the number of hours Marty worked last week.

2-3 Solving Two-Step and Multi-Step Equations

Solve each equation. Check your answer.

11. $-2a + 8 = 14$ 12. $8.5b - 6 = 53.5$ 13. $9 - \frac{1}{4}c = \frac{3}{8}$ 14. $5d + 24 = -36$

15. A car can be rented for \$45 plus \$0.14 per mile. Tammy paid \$63.90. Write and solve an equation to show how many miles Tammy drove.

2-4 Solving Equations with Variables on Both Sides

Solve each equation. Check your answer.

16. $a + 15 = -4a$ **17.** $0.45b = 2.25b - 9$ **18.** $\frac{3}{5}c - \frac{1}{5} = \frac{1}{10}c$ **19.** $-2d - 14 = -4 + d$

2-5 Solving for a Variable

20. Solve $p = 4 - m$ for m.

21. Solve $ab = 8 - c$ for a.

22. Solve $mn - 3 = s$ for n.

23. Solve $\frac{d - 5}{f} = g$ for f.

24. The formula for the perimeter of a rectangle is $P = 2l + 2w$, where l is the length and w is the width. Solve for w.

2-6 Rates, Ratios, and Proportions

Solve each proportion.

25. $\frac{6}{d} = \frac{2}{16}$

26. $\frac{t}{5} = \frac{25}{20}$

27. $\frac{0.5}{1.5} = \frac{2.5}{m - 0.5}$

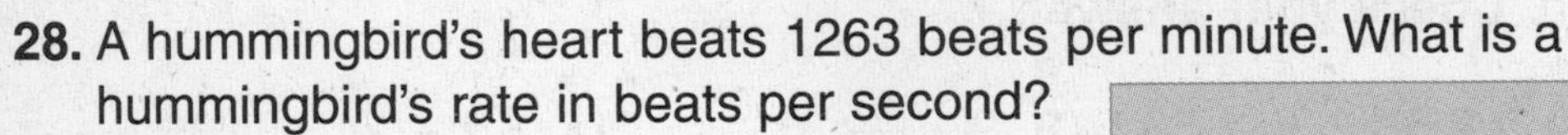

28. A hummingbird's heart beats 1263 beats per minute. What is a hummingbird's rate in beats per second?

2-7 Applications of Proportions

29. Every dimension of a cube with length 4 inches is multiplied by 1.5 to get a similar cube. How is the ratio of the volumes related to the ratio of the corresponding dimensions?

30. A firefighter who is 6.5 feet tall casts a shadow 4 feet long. At the same time,a building cast a shadow 54 feet. Write and solve a proportion to find the height of the building.

2-8 Percents

Evaluate each expression for the given value of *x*.

31. Find 45% of 360.

32. What percent of 240 is 78?

33. 5 is what percent of 80?

34. 208% of what number is 312?

35. What percent of 72 is 5.4?

36. Find 8.5% of 240.

37. A certain glass of orange juice contains 12% of the recommended daily allowance of vitamin C. The recommended daily allowance is 60 mg. How many milligrams of vitamin C are in the glass of orange juice?

2-9 Applications of Percents

38. A car salesman earns a 3.5% commission on each car he sells. Find the commission earned when a car is sold for $25,500.

39. Find the amount of simple interest earned after 5 years on $1450 invested at a 1.5% annual interest rate.

40. Estimate the tip on a $38.90 check using a tip rate of 15%.

41. Find the total amount owed after 18 months on a loan of $84,500 at an annual interest rate of 6.5%.

42. Estimate the tax on a $108 calculator when the sales tax is 4.35%.

43. Find the number of years it would take for $1500 to earn simple interest of $945 at an annual rate of 2.25%.

44. The simple interest paid on a loan after 9 months was $702. The annual interest rate was 6%. Find the principal.

2-10 Percent Increase and Decrease

Find each percent change. Tell whether it is a percent increase or decrease.

45. from 50 to 86 **46.** from 125 to 75 **47.** from 24 to 6 **48.** from 14 to 70

49. Sallie purchased a travel bag that had a 30% markup. The wholesale cost was $25. What was the selling price?

50. Steve uses a coupon and paid $52.50 for a watch that normally costs $75.00. What is the percent discount?

Big Ideas

Answer these questions to summarize the important concepts from Chapter 2 in your own words.

1. Explain how the four properties of equality help you solve equations.

2. Explain the difference between an identity and a contradiction.

3. What are the steps for solving for a variable?

4. Explain how you can solve a proportion for a missing value.

5. Explain how to find a percent change.

For more review of Chapter 2:

- Complete the Chapter 2 Study Guide and Review on pages 152–155 of your textbook.
- Complete the Ready to Go On quizzes on pages 113 and 147 of your textbook.

Vocabulary

The table contains important vocabulary terms from Chapter 3. As you work through the chapter, fill in the page number, definition, and a clarifying example for each term.

Term	Page	Definition	Clarifying Example
compound inequality			
inequality			
intersection			

Term	Page	Definition	Clarifying Example
solution of an inequality			
Union			

LESSON 3-1

Graphing and Writing Inequalities

Lesson Objectives

Identify solutions of inequalities in one variable; Write and graph inequalities in one variable

Vocabulary

inequality (p. 168) ______________________________

____

solution of an inequality (p. 168): ______________________________

____

Key Concepts

Graphing Inequalities (p. 169):

WORDS	ALGEBRA	GRAPH
All real numbers less than 5		−4 −3 −2 −1 0 1 2 3 4 5 6
All real numbers greater than −1		−4 −3 −2 −1 0 1 2 3 4 5 6
All real numbers less than or equal to $\frac{1}{2}$		−2 $-1\frac{1}{2}$ −1 $-\frac{1}{2}$ 0 $\frac{1}{2}$ 1
All real numbers greater than or equal to 0		−4 −3 −2 −1 0 1 2 3 4 5 6

Think and Discuss (p. 170)

Get Organized Draw a graph in the first row and write the correct inequality in the second row.

Inequality	Graph
	−5 −4 −3 −2 −1 0 1

LESSON 3-2

Solving One-Step Inequalities by Adding or Subtracting

Lesson Objectives

Solve one-step inequalities by using addition; Solve one-step inequalities by using subtraction

Key Concepts

Properties of Inequality (p. 174):

Addition and Subtraction		
WORDS	**NUMBERS**	**ALGEBRA**
Addition You can add the same number to both sides of an inequality, and the statement will still be true.	$3 < 8$ $3 + 2 < 8 + 2$ $5 < 10$	$a < b$ $a + c < b + c$
Subtraction You can subtract the same number from both sides of an inequality, and the statement will still be true.	$9 < 12$ $9 - 5 < 12 - 5$ $4 < 7$	$a < b$ $a - c < b - c$
These properties are also true for inequalities that use the symbols $>$, $\geq$, and $\leq$.		

Get Organized In each box, write an inequality that requires the specified property to be solved. Then solve and graph the inequality.

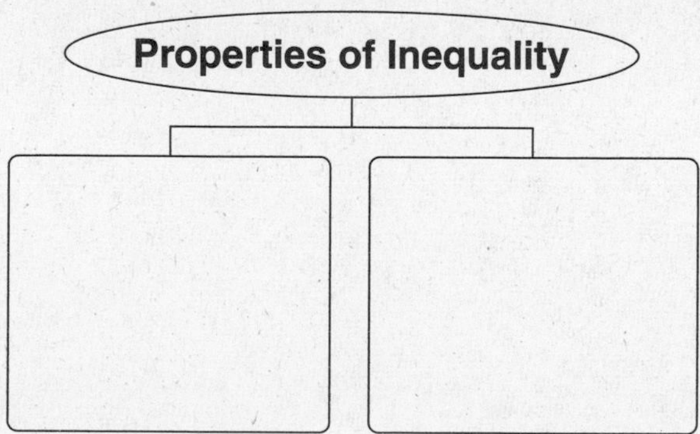

LESSON 3-3

Solving One-Step Inequalities by Multiplying or Dividing

Lesson Objectives

Solve one-step inequalities by using multiplication; Solve one-step inequalities by using division

Key Concepts

Properties of inequality (p. 180):

Multiplication and Division by Positive Numbers		
WORDS	**NUMBERS**	**ALGEBRA**
Multiplication		
Division		
These properties are also true for inequalities that use the symbols >, ≥, and ≤.		

Properties of Inequality (p. 181):

Multiplication and Division by Negative Numbers		
WORDS	**NUMBERS**	**ALGEBRA**
Multiplication If you multiply both sides of an inequality by the same *negative* number, you must reverse the inequality symbol for the statement to still be true.	$8 > 4$ $8(-2)$ ▆ $4(-2)$ -16 ▆ -8 $-16 < -8$	If $a > b$ and $c < 0$, then $ac < bc$.
Division If you divide both sides of an inequality by the same *negative* number, you must reverse the inequality symbol for the statement to still be true.	$12 > 4$ $\frac{12}{-4}$ ▆ $\frac{4}{-4}$ -3 ▆ -1 $-3 < -1$	If $a > b$ and $c < 0$, then $\frac{a}{c} < \frac{b}{c}$.
These properties are also true for inequalities that use the symbols >, ≥, and ≤.		

Think and Discuss (p. 182)

Get Organized In each cell, write and solve an inequality.

Solving Inequalities by Using Multiplication and Division		
	By a Positive Number	**By a Negative Number**
Divide		
Multiply		

LESSON 3-4

Solving Two-Step and Multi-Step Inequalities

Lesson Objectives

Solve inequalities that contain more than one operation

Key Concepts

Think and Discuss (p. 190)

Get Organized Complete the graphic organizer.

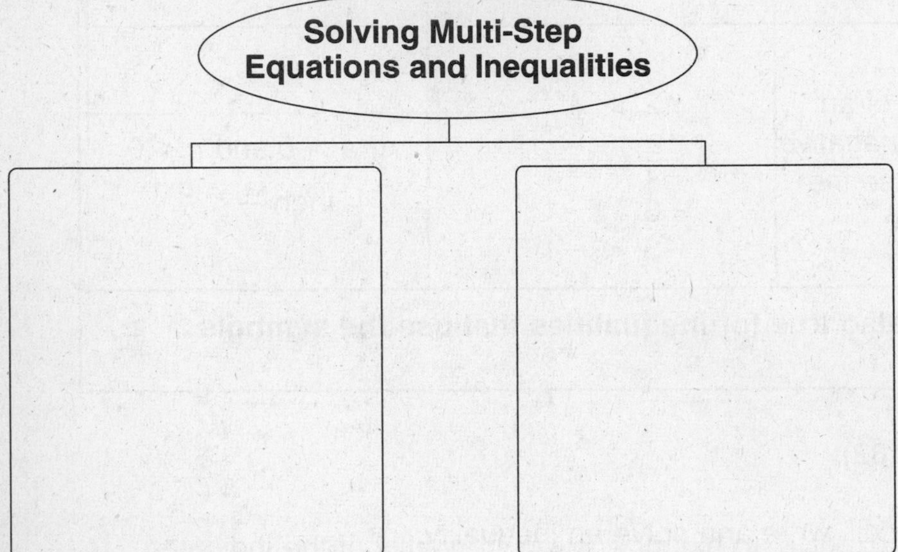

LESSON 3-5

Solving Inequalities with Variables on Both Sides

Know it! Note

Lesson Objectives

Solve inequalities that contain variable terms on both sides

Key Concepts

Identities and Contradictions (p. 196):

WORDS	ALGEBRA
Identity	
Contradiction	
These properties are also true for inequalities that use the symbols >, ≥, and ≤.	

Think and Discuss (p. 197)

Get Organized In each box, give an example of an inequality of the indicated type.

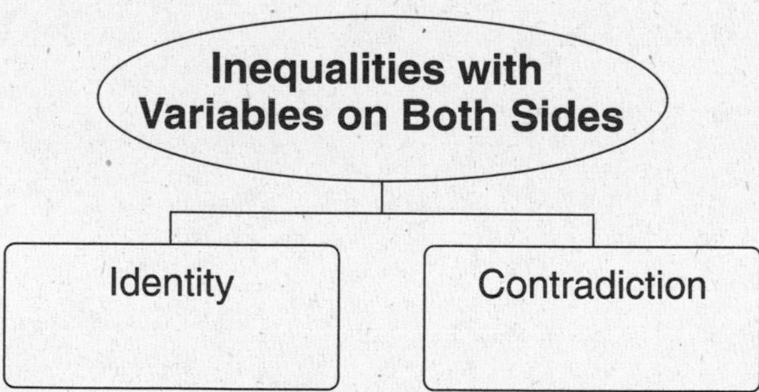

LESSON 3-6

Solving Compound Inequalities

Lesson Objectives

Solve compound inequalities in one variable; Graph solution sets of compound inequalities in one variable

Vocabulary

compound inequality (p. 202): ______________________________

____

intersection (p. 203): ______________________________

____

union (p. 204): ______________________________

____

Key Concepts

Compound Inequalities (p. 202):

WORDS	ALGEBRA	GRAPH
All real numbers greater than 2 AND less than 6		
All real numbers greater than or equal to 2 AND less than or equal to 6		
All real numbers less than 2 OR greater than 6		
All real numbers less than or equal to 2 OR greater than or equal to 6		

Think and Discuss (p. 205)

Get Organized Write three solutions in each of the three sections of the diagram. Then write each of your nine solutions in the appropriate column or columns of the table.

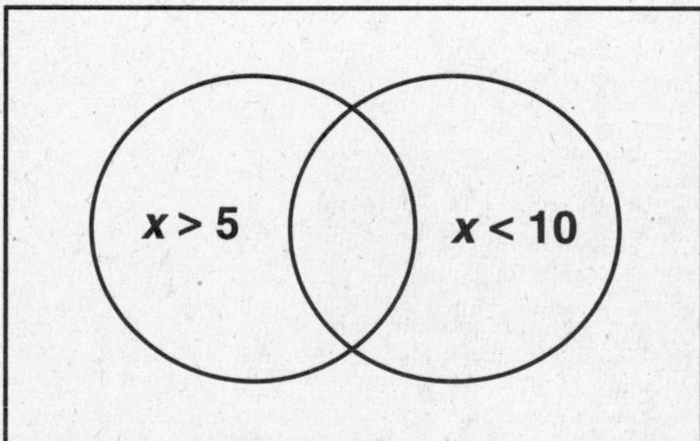

$x > 5$ AND $x < 10$	$x > 5$ OR $x < 10$

Chapter Review

3-1 Graphing and Writing Inequalities

Write the inequality shown by each graph.

1. 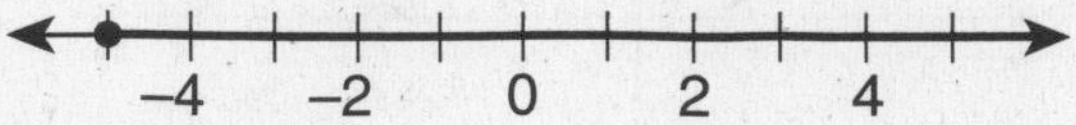

2. 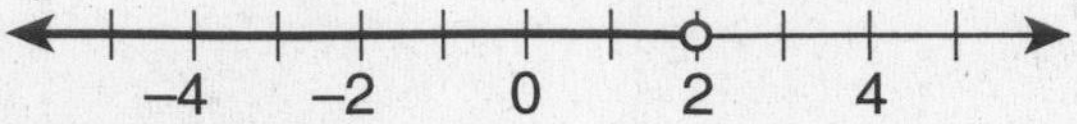

3. 

Graph each inequality.

4. $r \geq -1$

5. $g < 2^2$

3-2 Solving One-Step Inequalities by Adding and Subtracting

Solve each inequality and graph the solutions.

6. $4 \geq t - 3$

7. $r + 7 < 12$

8. Danny must have at least 410 points to receive an A. He has 275 points. Write and solve an inequality to show the least number of points Danny needs to receive an A.

3-3 Solving One-Step Inequalities by Multiplying and Dividing

Solve each inequality and graph the solutions.

9. $\frac{k}{3} \leq 2$

10. $3 > \frac{h}{-2}$

11. $-2r < -6$

12. Hannah wants to buy 4 presents for at least \$60. She wants to spend an equal amount of money on each present. Write and solve an inequality to show the least amount of money Hannah will spend on each present.

3-4 Solving Two-Step and Multi-Step Inequalities

Solve each inequality.

13. $c + 3c > 2 + 14$

14. $2^3 + 12 \leq 2r - 12r$

15. $14 < \frac{6 - 2f}{2}$

16. $\frac{1}{3}b - \frac{1}{2} \geq \frac{5}{6}$

Solve each inequality and graph the solutions.

17. $-5a + 2 \geq 22$

18. $13 < 2t - 3(t - 3)$

3-5 Solving Inequalities with Variables on Both Sides

Solve each inequality.

19. $\frac{1}{2}(3 - 8t) > 20(1 - \frac{1}{5}t)$

20. $2(4 - a) - 2 \leq -2a + 6$

Solve each inequality and graph the solutions.

21. $4(3m - 1) \geq 2(m + 3)$

22. $9d - 4 \geq 12 + 5d$

23. The booster club raised \$104 to buy soccer balls for the soccer team. Each soccer ball costs \$19. How many soccer balls can the booster club buy?

3-6 Solving Compound Inequalities

Solve each compound inequality and graph the solutions.

24. $-4 < r - 5 \leq -1$

25. $4v + 3 < -5$ or $-2v + 7 < 1$

Write the compound inequality shown by each graph.

26.

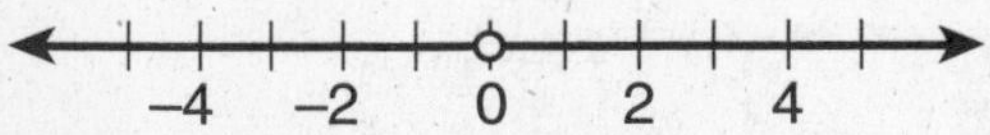

27.

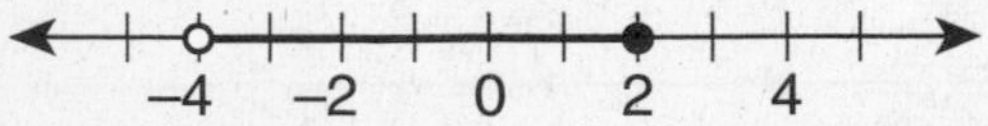

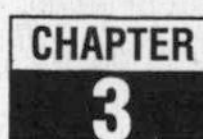

Big Ideas

Answer these questions to summarize the important concepts from Chapter 3 in your own words.

1. Explain how to show that an endpoint is a solution. Explain how to show that an endpoint is not a solution.

2. Explain how solving a one-step or multi-step inequality is like solving a one-step or multi-step equation.

3. Explain how solving inequalities by multiplying or dividing by a negative number is different from solving inequalities by multiplying or dividing by a positive number.

4. Explain how to graph a compound inequality involving a union

For more review of Chapter 3:

- Complete the Chapter 3 Study Guide and Review on pages 216–219 of your textbook.
- Complete the Ready to Go On quizzes on pages 187 and 211 of your textbook.

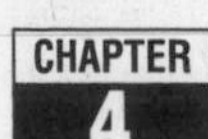

Vocabulary

This table contains important vocabulary terms from Chapter 4. As you work through the chapter, fill in the page number, definition, and a clarifying example for each term.

Term	Page	Definition	Clarifying Example
arithmetic sequence			
continuous graph			
correlation			
dependent variable			
discrete graph			
domain			
function			
function notation			
function rule			
independent variable			

Term	Page	Definition	Clarifying Example
negative correlation			
no correlation			
positive correlation			
range			
relation			
scatter plot			
sequence			

Graphing Relationships

Lesson Objectives

Match simple graphs with situations; Graph a relationship

Vocabulary

continuous graph (p. 231): ______________________________

____

discrete graph (p. 231): ______________________________

____

Key Concepts

Think and Discuss (p. 232)

Get Organized Write an example of key words that suggest the given segments on a graph. One example of each segment is given for you.

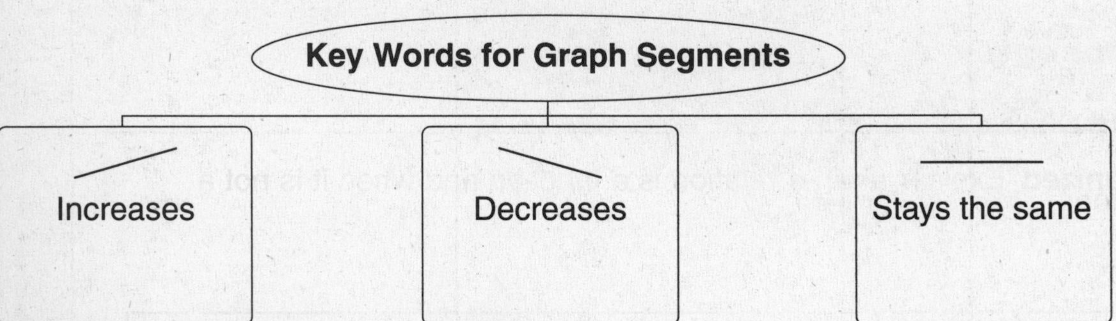

Relations and Functions

Lesson Objectives

Identify functions; Find the domain and range of relations and functions

Vocabulary

relation (p. 236): ______________________________

____

domain (p. 236): ______________________________

____

range (p. 236): ______________________________

____

function (p. 237): ______________________________

____

Key Concepts

Think and Discuss (p. 238)

Get Organized Explain when a relation is a function and when it is not a function.

A relation is...	
A function if...	Not a function if...

Writing Function Rules

Lesson Objectives

Identify independent and dependent variables; Write an equation in function notation and evaluate a function for given input values

Vocabulary

independent variable (p. 246): ______________________________

____

dependent variable (p. 246): ______________________________

____

function rule (p. 246): ______________________________

____

function notation (p. 247): ______________________________

____

Key Concepts

Think and Discuss (p. 248)

Get Organized Use the rule $y = x + 3$ and the domain $\{-2, -2, 0, 1, 2\}$.

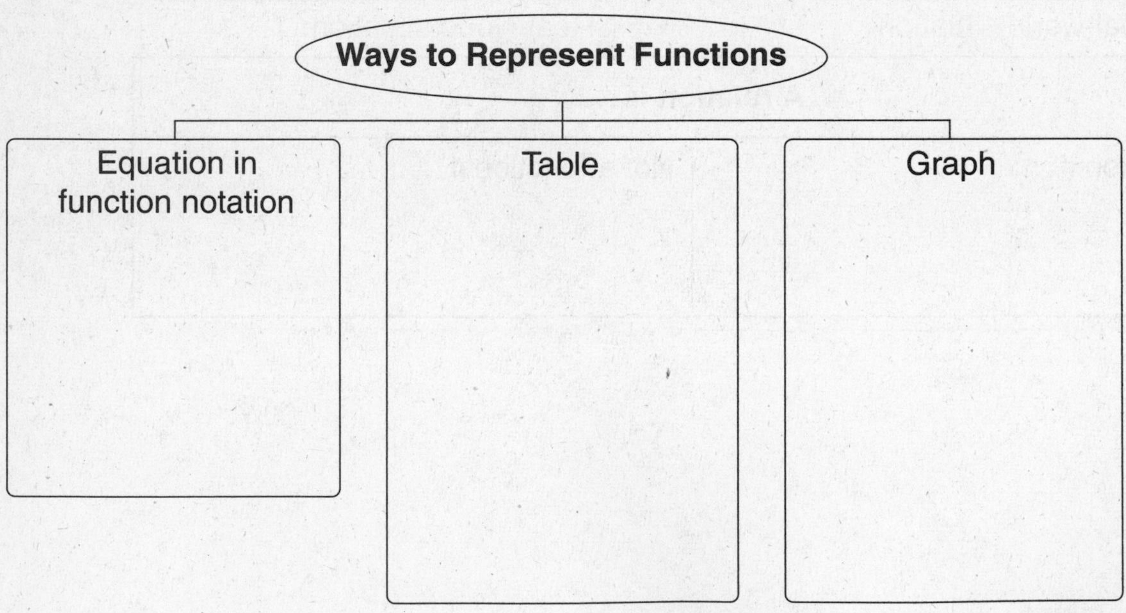

Graphing Functions

Lesson Objectives

Graph functions given a limited domain; Graph functions given a domain of all real numbers

Key Concepts

Graphing Functions Using a Domain of All Real Numbers (p. 253):

Graphing Functions Using a Domain of All Real Numbers
Step 1
Step 2
Step 3

Think and Discuss (p. 256)

Get Organized Explain how to graph a function for each situation.

An equation with variables on both sides can have...

Not a real-world situation:	Real-world situation:

Scatter Plots and Trend Lines

Lesson Objectives

Create and interpret scatter plots; Use trend lines to make predictions

Vocabulary

scatter plot (p. 262): ______

correlation (p. 262): ______

positive correlation (p. 263): ______

negative correlation (p. 263): ______

no correlation (p. 263): ______

trend line (p. 265): ______

Key Concepts

Correlations (p. 263):

Correlations		
Positive Correlation	**Negative Correlation**	**No Correlation**

Think and Discuss (p. 265)

Get Organized Complete the graphic organizer with either a scatter plot, or a real-world example, or both.

	GRAPH	EXAMPLE
Positive Correlation		
Negative Correlation		
No Correlation		

Arithmetic Sequences

Lesson Objectives

Recognize and extend an arithmetic sequence; Find a given term of an arithmetic sequence

Vocabulary

sequence (p. 272): ______________________________

____

term (p. 272): ______________________________

____

arithmetic sequence (p. 272): ______________________________

____

common difference (p. 272): ______________________________

____

Key Concepts

Finding the *n*th Term of an Arithmetic Sequence (p. 273):

Finding the *n*th Term of an Arithmetic Sequence

Think and Discuss (p. 274)

Get Organized Complete the graphic organizer with steps for finding the *n*th term of an arithmetic sequence.

Finding the *n*th Term of an Arithmetic Sequence → 1. → 2.

Chapter Review

4-1 Graphing Relationships

Choose the graph that best represents each situation.

1. A person runs a marathon at a constant rate of speed.

2. A person jogs, slows down when approaching a crosswalk, stops for traffic, and then starts to jog again.

3. A person suddenly gets chased by a dog while jogging.

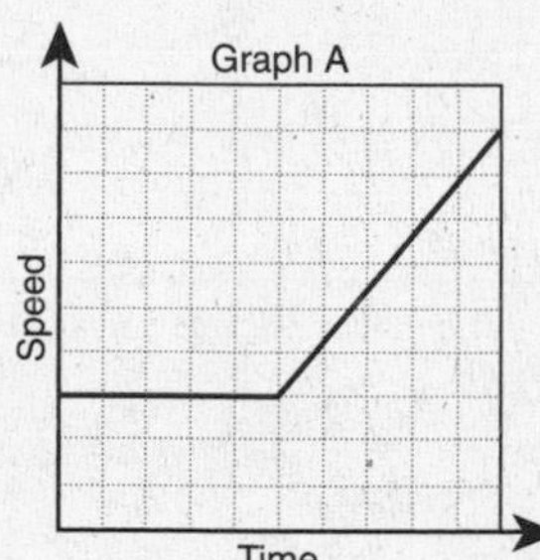

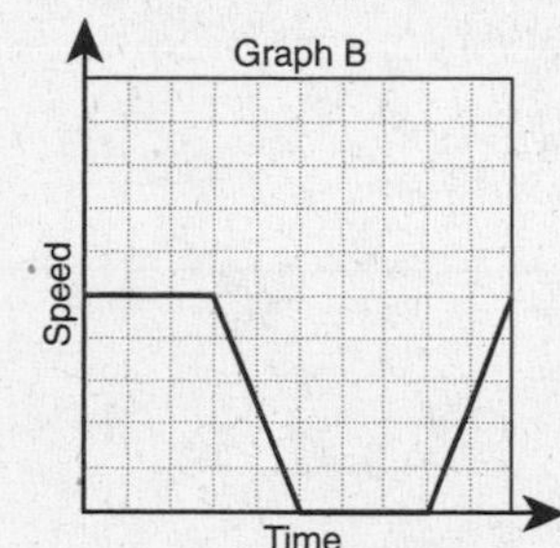

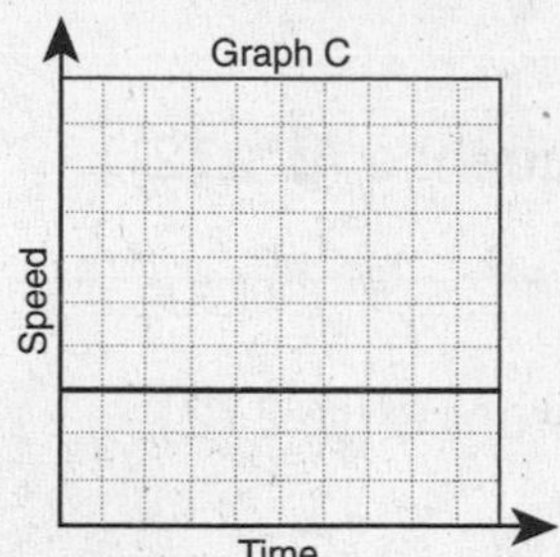

Write a possible situation for the graph.

4.

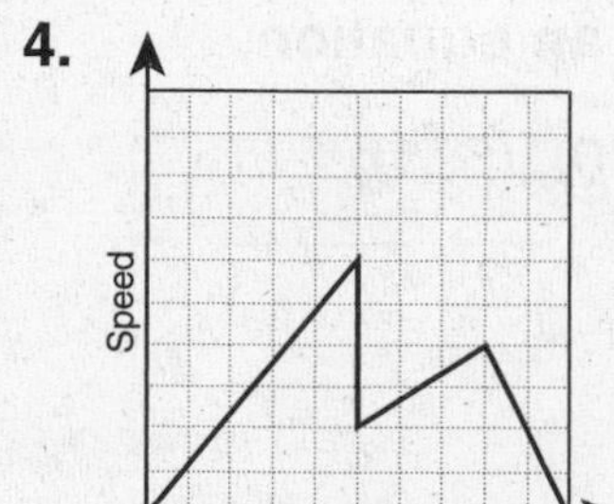

4-2 Relations and Functions

Give the domain and range of each relation. Tell whether the relation is a function. Explain.

5.

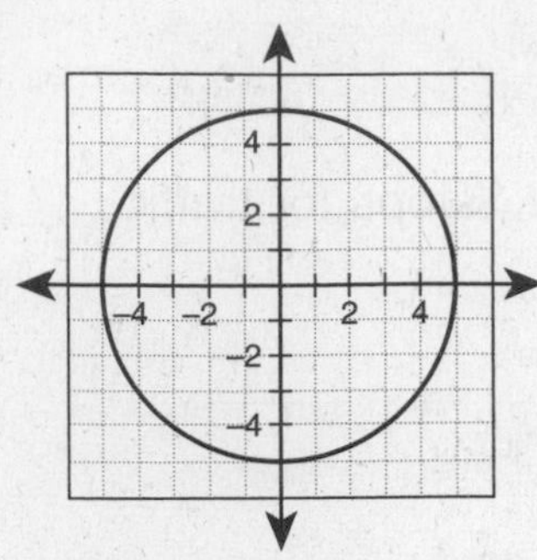

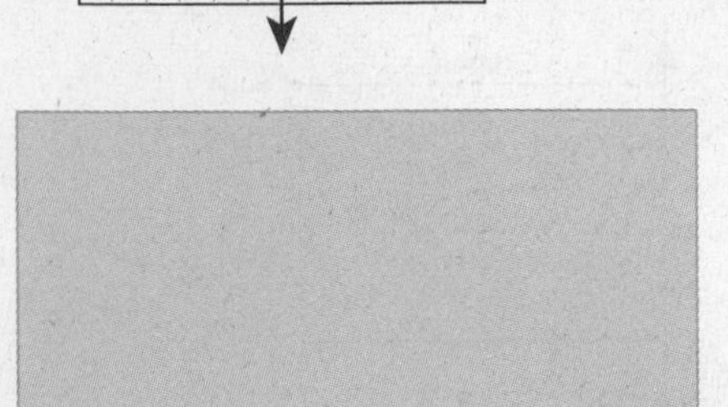

6. $\{(7, -7), (7, -7), (0, 0), (-7, 7), (-7, 7)\}$

4-3 Writing Function Rules

Determine a relationship between the *x*- and *y*-values. Write an equation.

7.

x	1	2	3	4
y	0	2	4	6

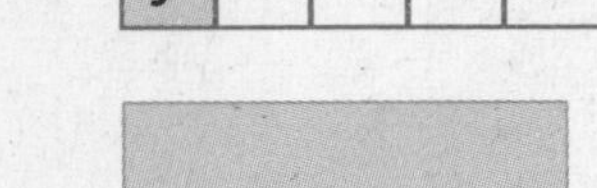

8. $\{(2, -2), (4, -1), (6, 0), (8, 1)\}$

Identify the dependant and independent variables. Write a rule in function notation for each situation.

9. An Internet music web site charges \$10 for a membership fee plus \$0.99 for each song download.

10. Mailing a letter costs $0.10 per ounce.

4-4 Graphing Functions

Graph each function for the given domain.

11. $f(x) = 3x - 1$; D: $\{-3, -1, 1, 3, 5\}$ **12.** $x^2 - y = 4$; D: $\{-2, -1, 0, 1, 2\}$

Graph each function.

13. $y = -\frac{1}{3}x - 1$

14. $y = 4x + 2$

4-5 Scatter Plots and Trend Lines

Choose the scatter plot that best represents the described relationship. Explain.

15. mathematics test score and number of hours studying

16. mathematics test score and number of missed test questions

17. mathematics test score and number of hours at volleyball practice

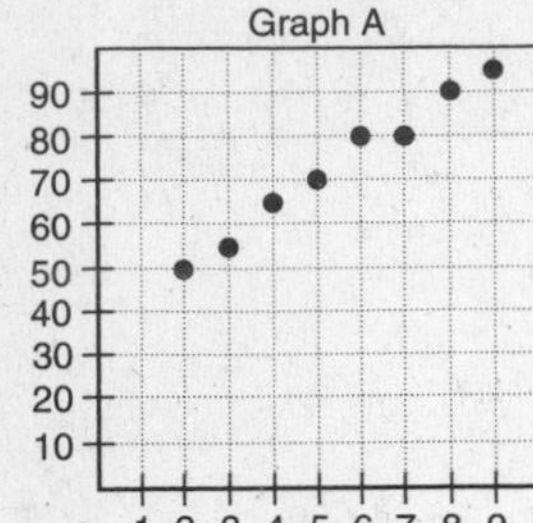

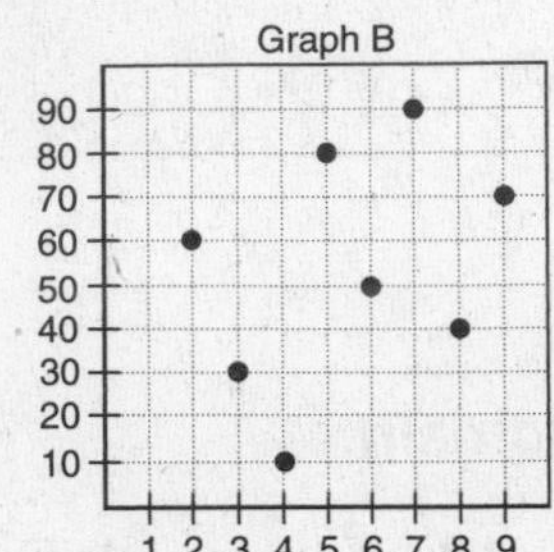

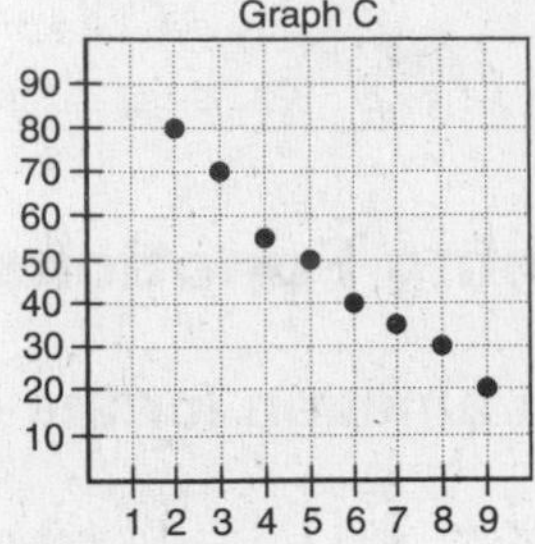

Identify the correlation you would expect to see between each pair of data sets. Explain.

18. The temperature of hot coffee and the amount of time a cup of coffee sits on a desk.

19. The length of your hair and the amount of rain that fell in May.

4-6 Arithmetic Sequences

Determine whether each sequence appears to be an arithmetic sequence. If so, find the common difference and the next three terms.

20. $-12.5, -10, -7.5, -5, \ldots$

21. $20, 10, -20, -10, \ldots$

22. $1\frac{1}{2}, 2\frac{1}{4}, 3, 3\frac{3}{4}, \ldots$

Find the indicated term of the arithmetic sequence.

23. $-11, -14, -17, -20, \ldots$; 13th term

24. $-6, -2, 2, 6, \ldots$; 31st term

Big Ideas

Answer these questions to summarize the important concepts from Chapter 4 in your own words.

1. Explain the difference between a continuous graph and a discrete graph. Give an example of continuous data and discrete data.

2. Explain when a relation is a function.

3. Explain the difference between an independent variable and a dependent variable.

4. Explain how to graph a function using a domain of all real numbers.

5. Write about a situation where you would expect the correlation to be negative.

6. Explain how to find the *n*th term of an arithmetic sequence.

For more review of Chapter 4:

- Complete the Chapter 4 Study Guide and Review on pages 280–283.
- Compete the Ready to Go On quizzes on pages 261 and 279.

Vocabulary

This table contains important vocabulary terms from Chapter 5. As you work through the chapter, fill in the page number, definition, and a clarifying example for each term.

Term	Page	Definition	Clarifying Example
constant of variation			
direct variation			
family of functions			
linear equation			
linear function			
parallel lines			
perpendicular lines			

Term	Page	Definition	Clarifying Example
rate of change			
reflection			
rise			
rotation			
run			
slope			
transformation			
translation			

Identifying Linear Functions

Lesson Objectives

Identify linear functions and linear equations; Graph linear functions that represent real-world situations and give their domain and range

Vocabulary

linear function (p. 296): ______________________________

____

linear equation (p. 298): ______________________________

____

Key Concepts

Standard Form of a Linear Equation (p. 298):

Think and Discuss (p. 299)

Get Organized In each box, describe how to use the information to identify a linear function. Include an example.

Determining Whether a Function is Linear

From its graph	From its equation	From a list of ordered pairs

Using Intercepts

Know it!
Note

Lesson Objectives

Find *x*- and *y*-intercepts and interpret their meanings in real-world situations; Use *x*- and *y*-intercepts to graph lines

Vocabulary

y-intercept (p. 303): ______________________________

____

x-intercept (p. 303): ______________________________

____

Key Concepts

Think and Discuss (p. 305)

Get Organized Complete the graphic organizer.

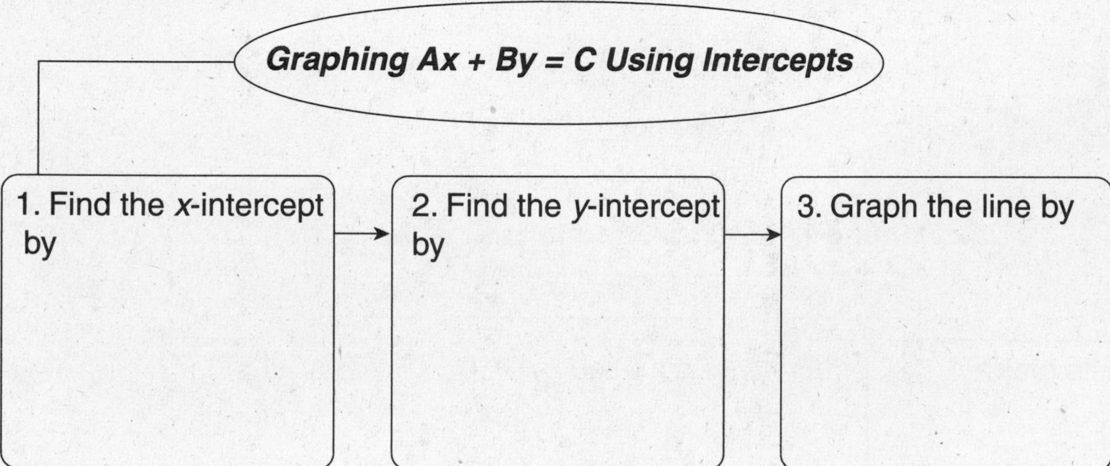
Graphing Ax + By = C Using Intercepts
1. Find the x-intercept by
2. Find the y-intercept by
3. Graph the line by

LESSON 5-3

Rate of Change and Slope

Lesson Objectives

Find rates of change and slopes; Relate a constant rate of change to the slope of a line

Vocabulary

rate of change (p. 310) ______________________________

____

rise (p. 311): ______________________________

____

run (p. 311): ______________________________

____

slope (p. 311): ______________________________

____

Key Concepts

Slope of a Line (p. 311):

Positive, Negative, Zero, and Undefined Slope (p. 312):

Think and Discuss (p. 313)

Get Organized In each box, sketch a line whose slope matches the given description.

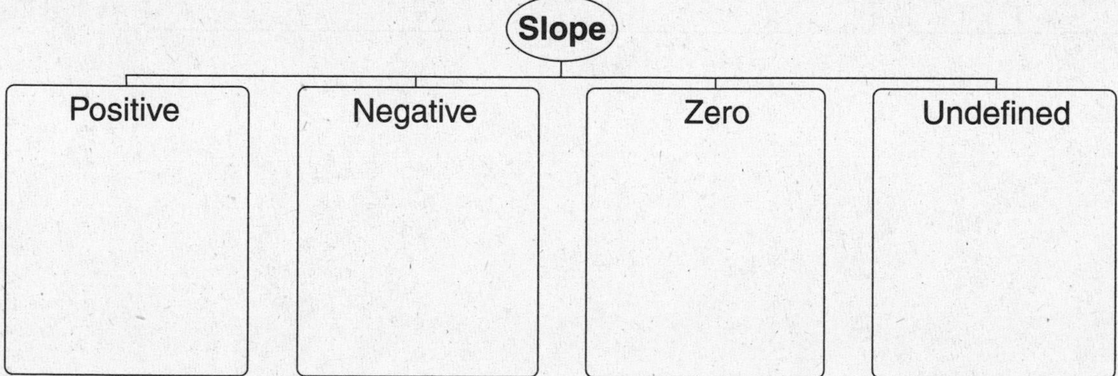

The Slope Formula

Lesson Objectives

Find the slope by using the slope formula

Key Concepts

Slope Formula (p. 320):

WORDS	FORMULA	EXAMPLE

Get Organized In each box, describe how to find slope using the given method.

Finding Slope

From a graph	From a table	From an equation

Direct Variation

Lesson Objectives

Identify, write, and graph direct variation

Vocabulary

direct variation (p. 326): ______________________________

____

constant of variation (p. 326): ______________________________

____

Key Concepts

Think and Discuss (p. 329)

Get Organized In each box, describe how you can use the given information to identify a direct variation.

Recognizing a Direct Variation		
From an Equation	From Ordered Pairs	From a Graph

LESSON
5-6

Slope-Intercept Form

Know it!
Note

Lesson Objectives

Write a linear equation in slope-intercept form; Graph a line using slope-intercept form

Key Concepts

Slope-Intercept Form of a Linear Equation (p. 335):

Think and Discuss (p. 337)

Get Organized Complete the graphic organizer.

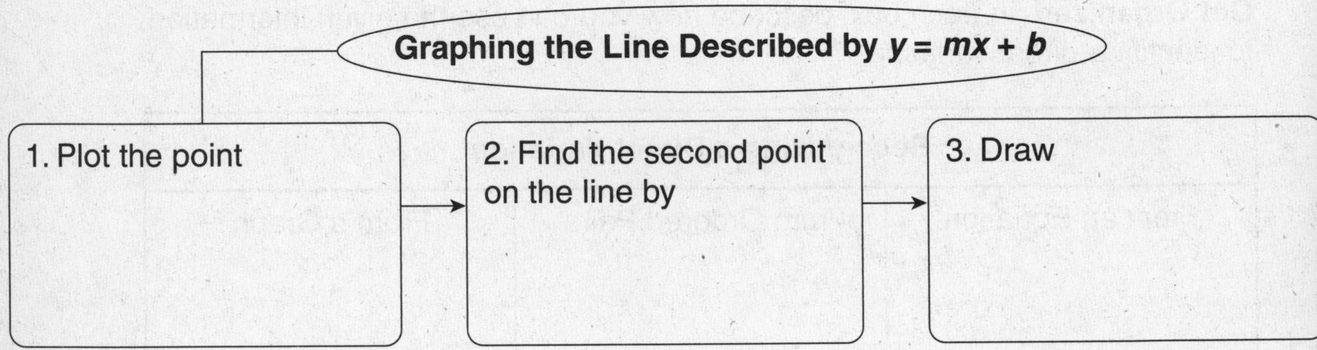
Graphing the Line Described by $y = mx + b$
1. Plot the point
2. Find the second point on the line by
3. Draw

Point-Slope Form

Lesson Objectives

Graph a line and write a linear equation using point-slope form; Write a linear equation given two points

Key Concepts

Point-Slope Form of a Linear Equation (p. 342)

Think and Discuss (p. 344)

Get Organized In each box, describe how to find the equation of a line by using the given method.

Writing the Equation of a Line

If you know two points on the line:	If you know the slope and y-intercept:	If you know the slope and a point on the line:

LESSON **5-8**

Slopes of Parallel and Perpendicular Lines

Lesson Objectives

Identify and graph parallel and perpendicular lines; Write equations to describe lines parallel or perpendicular to a given line

Vocabulary

parallel lines (p. 349) ______________________________

perpendicular lines (p. 351) ______________________________

Key Concepts

Parallel Lines (p. 349):

Perpendicular Lines (p. 351):

Think and Discuss (p. 352)

Get Organized In each box, sketch an example and describe the slopes.

Parallel lines	Perpendicular lines

LESSON 5-9

Transforming Linear Functions

Lesson Objectives

Describe how changing slope and y-intercept affect the graph of a linear function

Vocabulary

family of functions (p. 357): ______________________________

____

parent function (p. 357): ______________________________

____

transformation (p. 357): ______________________________

____

translation (p. 357): ______________________________

____

rotation (p. 358): ______________________________

____

reflection (p. 359): ______________________________

____

Key Concepts

Vertical Translation of a Linear Function (p. 357)

Rotation of a Linear Function (p. 358)

Reflection of a Linear Function (p. 359)

Think and Discuss (p. 360)

Get Organized In each box, sketch a graph of the given transformation of $f(x) = x$, and label it with a possible equation.

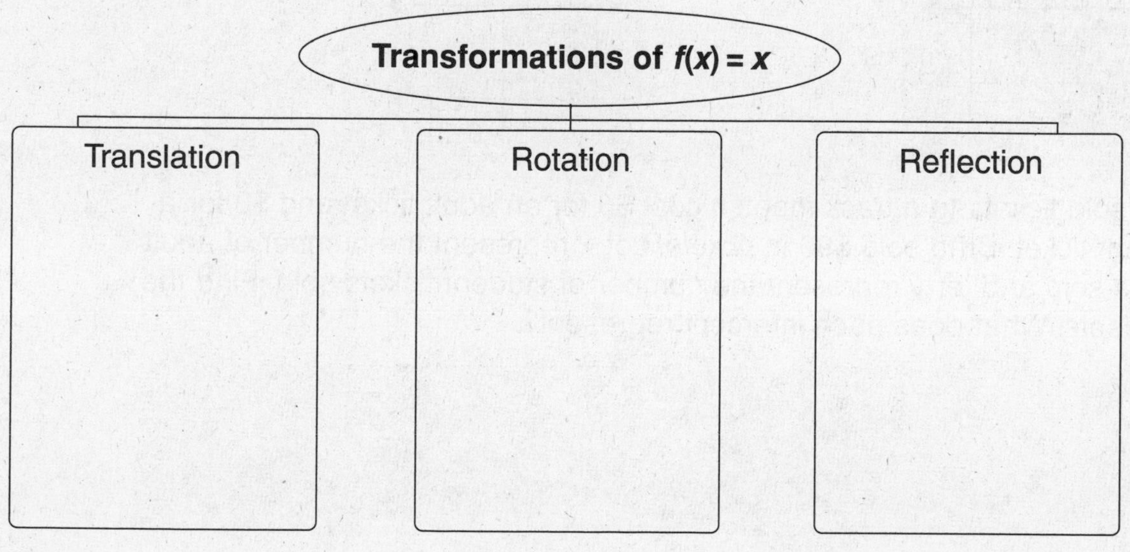

CHAPTER 5

Chapter Review

5-1 Identifying Linear Functions

Tell whether the given ordered pairs satisfy a linear function. Explain.

1. $\{(-4, 3), (-2, 2), (0, 1), (2, 0), (4, -1)\}$

2.

x	6	3	0	−3	−3
y	10	5	0	5	10

Tell whether each function is linear.

3. $x^3 - 2y + 3 = 0$

4. $9x - 3y = 6$

5-2 Using Intercepts

Use intercepts to graph the line described by each equation.

5. $2x + y = -4$

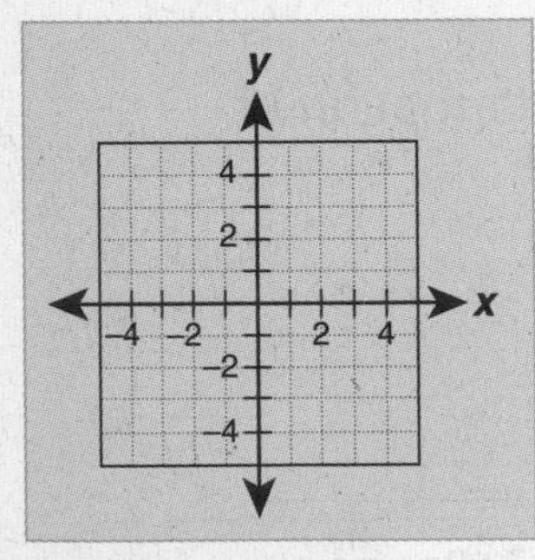

6. $3y - 12 = 1\frac{1}{2}x$

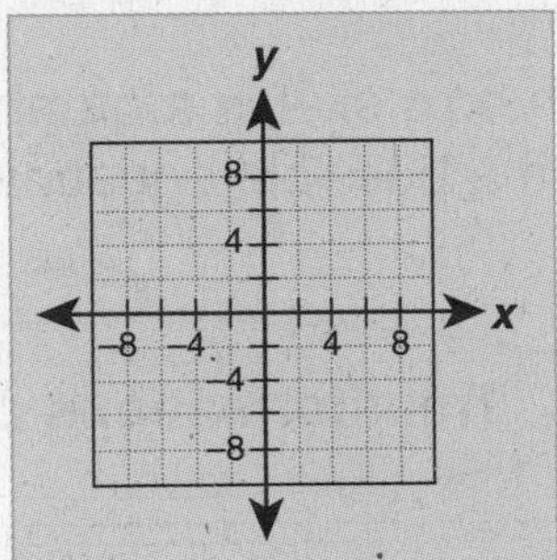

7. Brad sold tickets to a track meet. It cost \$6 for an adult ticket and \$3 for a student ticket. Brad sold \$90 in tickets. Let x represent the number of adult tickets sold and let y represent the number of student tickets sold. Find the intercepts. What does each intercept represent?

5-3 Rate of Change and Slope

Find the slope of each line.

8.

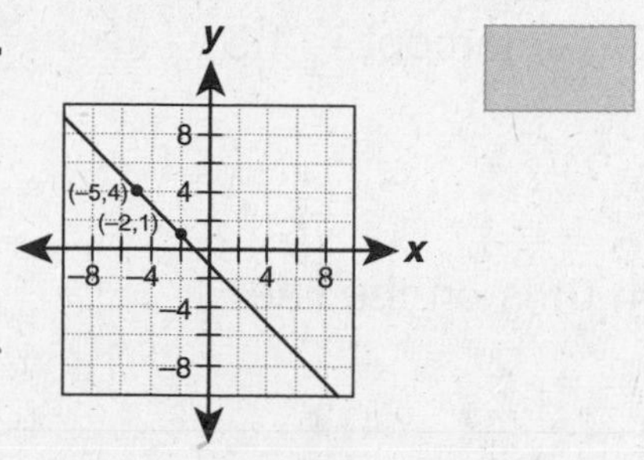

9.

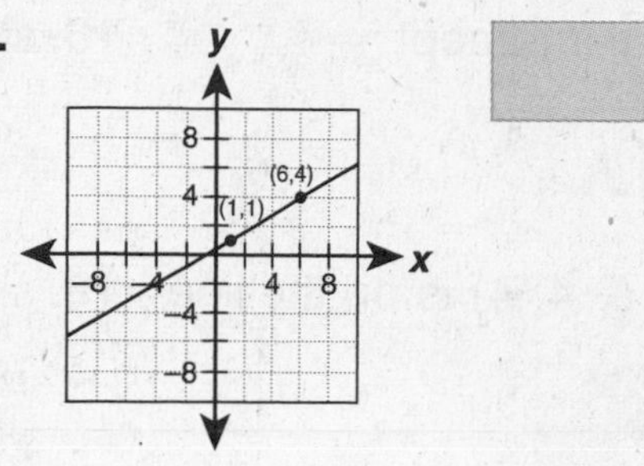

5-4 The Slope Formula

Find the slope of each line. Then tell what the slope represents.

10.

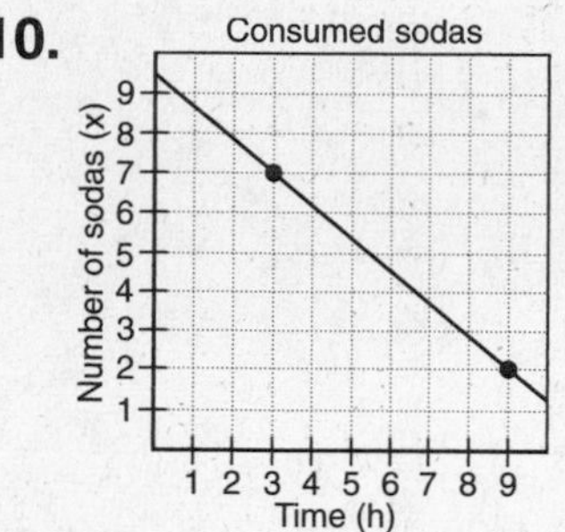

11.

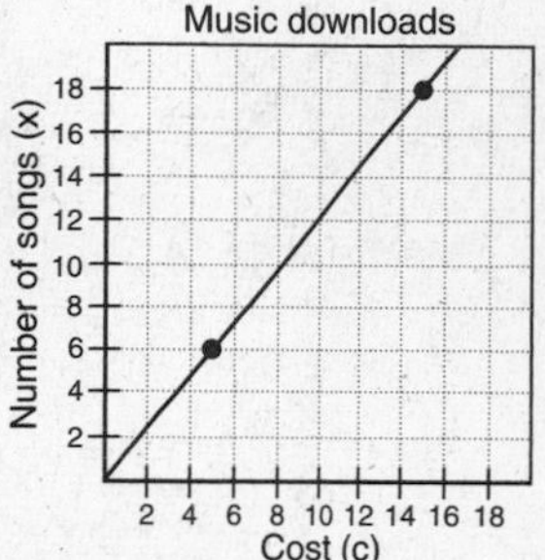

5-5 Direct Variation

Tell whether each relationship is a direct variation. If so, identify the constant of variation.

12.

x	−3	0	3	6
y	4	8	12	18

13.

x	−5	−2.5	0	2.5
y	−4	−2	0	2

14. The value of y varies directly with x, and $y = -6$ when $x = 3$. Find y when $x = 12$.

5-6 Slope-Intercept Form

Write the equation that describes each line in slope-intercept form.

15. slope = -3, y-intercept = 7

16. slope = 0.25, y-intercept = 1.5

17. slope = $-\frac{1}{6}$, $(-4, 4)$ is on the line

18. slope = 0, $(4, 0)$ is on the line

Write each equation in slope-intercept form. Then graph the line described by the equation.

19. $6x = 3y + 12$

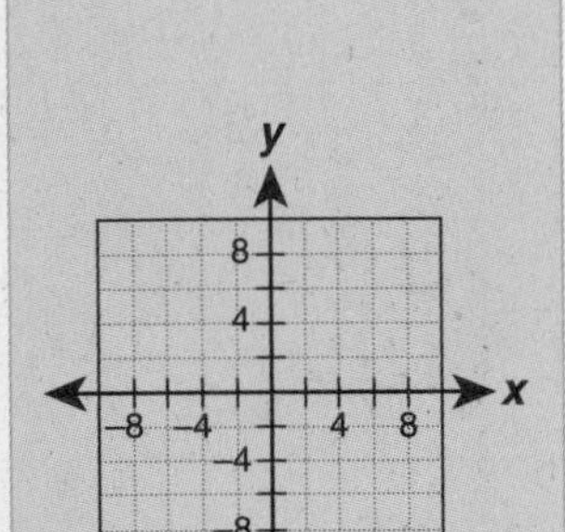

20. $-2x = 12 + 4y$

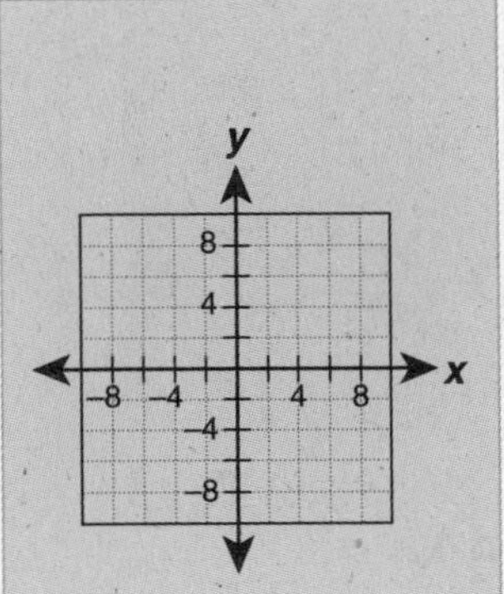

5-7 Point-Slope Form

Write an equation in slope-intercept form for the line through the two points.

21. $(-8, 2)$ and $(4, 3)$

22. $(0, 0)$ and $(6, 10)$

Graph the line with the given slope that contains the given point.

23. slope $= 2$; $(4, 2)$

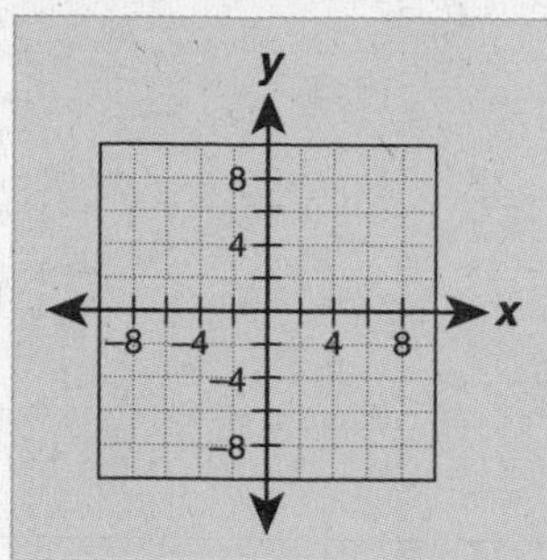

24. slope $= -\frac{1}{3}$; $(1, -3)$

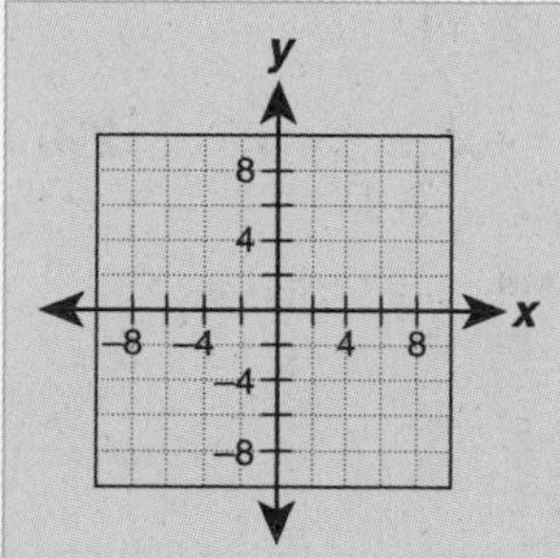

5-8 Slopes of Parallel and Perpendicular Lines

Identify which lines are parallel.

25. $y = 2(2x + 4)$; $y = 2x + 4$; $y = \frac{1}{2}(4x + 4)$; $y = 2(4x + 8)$

26. $y - \frac{1}{3} = 2x$; $y = \frac{1}{3}x + 2$; $y - \frac{1}{3} = \frac{2}{3}x + 2$; $y + \frac{1}{3} = \frac{1}{3}(6x + 2)$

27. Write an equation in slope-intercept form for the line that passes through $-3, 2$ and is perpendicular to the line described by $6x - 2y = 8$.

5-9 Transforming Linear Functions

Graph $f(x)$ and $g(x)$. Then describe the transformation(s) from the graph of $f(x)$ to the graph of $g(x)$.

28. $f(x) = 4x + 1$, $g(x) = x + 1$

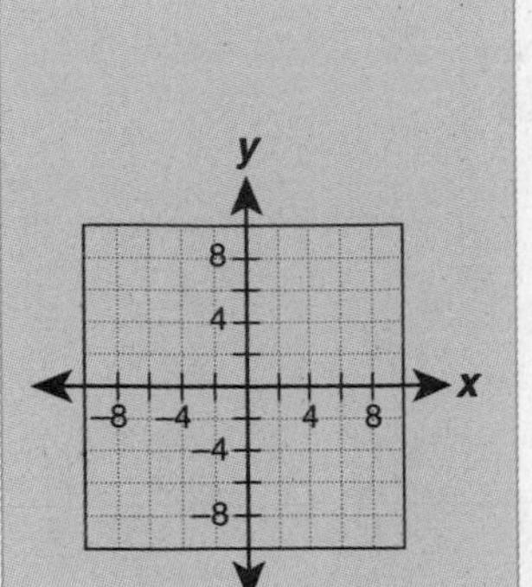

29. $f(x) = x + 4$, $g(x) = -x$

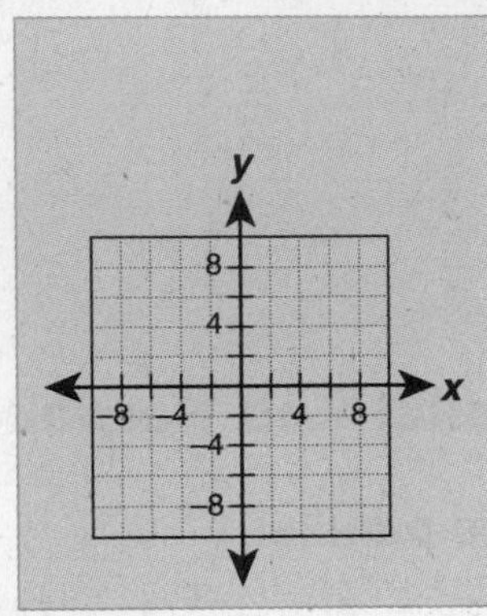

Big Ideas

Answer these questions to summarize the important concepts from Chapter 5 in your own words.

1. Explain how to find the x- and y-intercepts of a linear equation.

2. Explain how you can tell if the slope of a line is positive, negative, zero, or undefined by looking at a graph.

3. Explain the difference between slopes of parallel lines and slopes of perpendicular lines.

4. Explain how you can tell when a graph is translated, rotated, or reflected by looking at the equation of a linear function.

For more review of Chapter 5:

- Complete the Chapter 5 Study Guide and Review on pages 368–371 of your textbook.
- Compete the Ready to Go On quizzes on pages 333 and 365 of your textbook

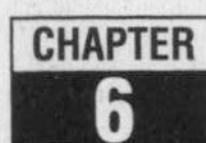

Vocabulary

This table contains important vocabulary terms from Chapter 6. As you work through the chapter, fill in the page number, definition, and a clarifying example for each term.

Term	Page	Definition	Clarifying Example
consistent system			
dependent system			
inconsistent system			
independent system			
linear inequality			
system of linear equations			

Term	Page	Definition	Clarifying Example
solution of a linear inequality			
solution of a system of linear equations			
solution of a system of linear inequalities			
system of linear inequalities			

LESSON 6-1

Solving Systems by Graphing

Lesson Objectives

Identify solutions of systems of linear equations in two variables; Solve systems of linear equations in two variables by graphing

Vocabulary

system of linear equations (p. 383) ______________________________

____

solution of a system of linear equations (p. 383) ______________________________

____

Key Concepts

Think and Discuss (p. 385)

Get Organized In each box, write a step for solving a linear system by graphing. More boxes may be added.

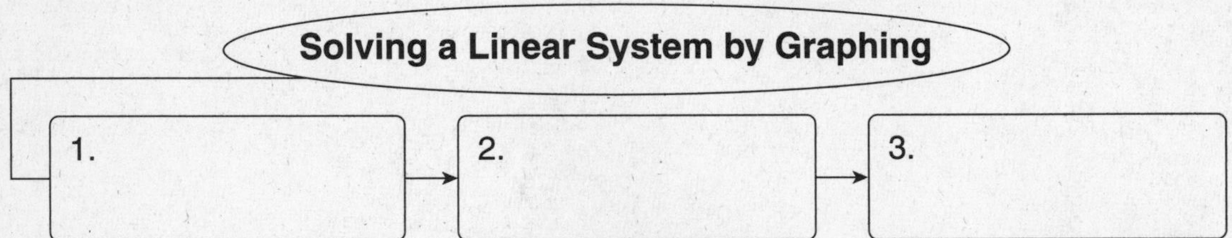

LESSON 6-2

Solving Systems by Substitution

Lesson Objectives

Solve systems of linear equations in two variables by substitution

Key Concepts

Solving Systems of Equations by Using Substitution (p. 390):

Solving Systems of Equations by Substitution
Step 1
Step 2
Step 3
Step 4
Step 5

Think and Discuss (p. 393)

Get Organized In each box, solve the system by substitution using the first step given. Show that each method gives the same solution.

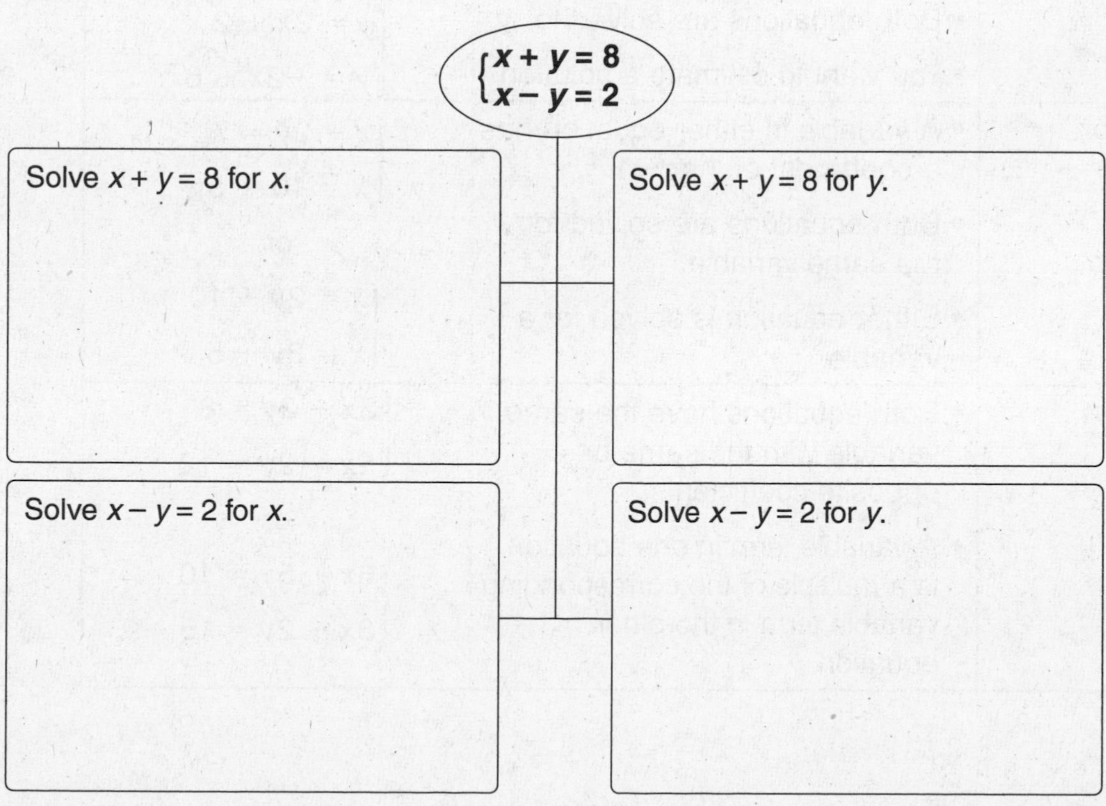

$\begin{cases} x + y = 8 \\ x - y = 2 \end{cases}$
Solve $x + y = 8$ for x.
Solve $x + y = 8$ for y.
Solve $x - y = 2$ for x.
Solve $x - y = 2$ for y.

LESSON 6-3

Solving Systems by Elimination

Lesson Objectives

Solve systems of linear equations in two variables by elimination; Compare and choose an appropriate method for solving systems of linear equations

Key Concepts

Solving Systems of Equations by Using Elimination (p. 397):

Solving Systems of Equations by Elimination
Step 1
Step 2
Step 3
Step 4

Systems of Linear Equations (p. 400):

METHOD	USE WHEN . . .	EXAMPLE
Graphing	• Both equations are solved for *y*. • You want to estimate a solution.	$\begin{cases} y = 3x + 2 \\ y = -2x + 6 \end{cases}$
Substitution	• A variable in either equation has a coefficient of 1 or −1. • Both equations are solved for the same variable. • Either equation is solved for a variable.	$\begin{cases} x + 2y = 7 \\ x = 10 - 5y \end{cases}$ or $\begin{cases} x = 2y + 10 \\ x = 3y + 5 \end{cases}$
Elimination	• Both equations have the same variable with the same or opposite coefficients. • A variable term in one equation is a multiple of the corresponding variable term in the other equation.	$\begin{cases} 3x + 2y = 8 \\ 5x + 2y = 12 \end{cases}$ or $\begin{cases} 6x + 5y = 10 \\ 3x + 2y = 15 \end{cases}$

Solving Systems of Equations by Substitution (p. 401)

Get Organized In each box, write an example of a system of equations that you could solve using the given method.

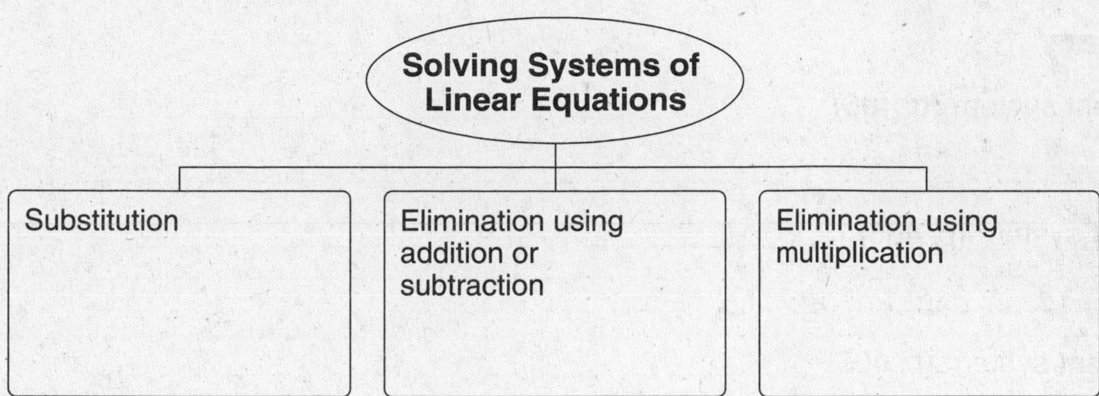

LESSON 6-4

Solving Special Systems

Lesson Objectives

Solve special systems of linear equations in two variables; Classify systems of linear equations and determine the number of solutions

Vocabulary

inconsistent system (p. 406) ________________________________

____

consistent system (p. 406) ________________________________

____

independent system (p. 407) ________________________________

____

dependent system (p. 407) ________________________________

Key Concepts

Classification of Systems of Linear Equations (p. 407):

CLASSIFICATION	CONSISTENT AND INDEPENDENT	CONSISTENT AND DEPENDENT	INCONSISTENT
Number of Solutions			
Description			
Graph			

Think and Discuss (p. 409)

Get Organized In each box, write the word that describes a system with that number of solutions and sketch a graph.

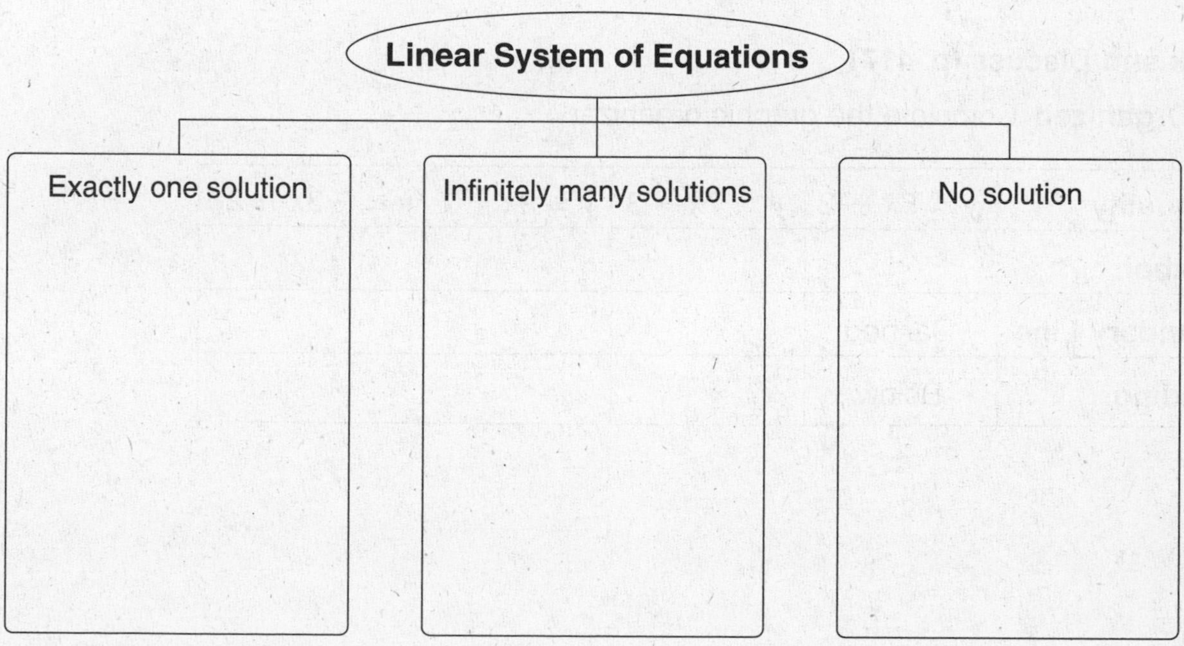

LESSON **6-5**

Solving for a Variable

Lesson Objectives

Graph and solve linear inequalities in two variables

Vocabulary

linear inequality (p. 414) ______________________________

____

solution of a linear inequality (p. 414) ______________________________

____

Key Concepts

Graphing Inequalities (p. 415):

Graphing Linear Inequalities	
Step 1	
Step 2	
Step 3	

Think and Discuss (p. 417)

Get Organized Complete the graphic organizer.

Inequality	$y < 5x + 2$	$y > 7x - 3$	$y \leq 9x + 1$	$y \geq -3x - 2$
Symbol	$<$			
Boundary Line	Dashed			
Shading	Below			

LESSON 6-6

Solving Systems of Linear Inequalities

Lesson Objectives

Graph and solve systems of linear inequalities in two variables

Vocabulary

system of linear inequalities (p. 421) ____________________

____

solution of a system of linear inequalities (p. 421) ____________________

____

Key Concepts

Think and Discuss (p. 423)

Get Organized In each box, draw a graph and list one solution.

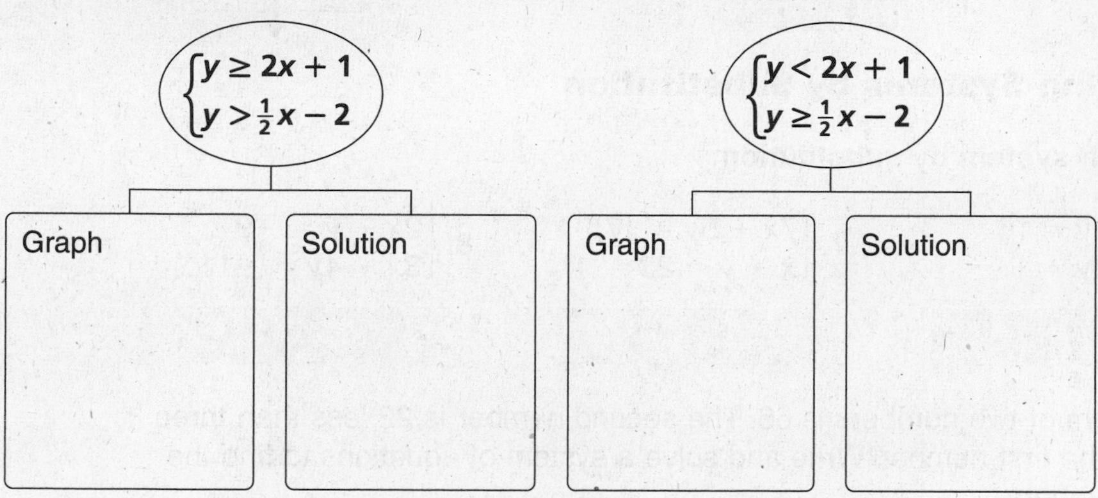

CHAPTER 6

Chapter Review

6-1 Solving Systems by Graphing

Tell whether the ordered pair is a solution of the given system.

1. $(2, -3)$; $\begin{cases} 2x - y = 7 \\ x - 2y = -5 \end{cases}$

2. $(-1, -5)$; $\begin{cases} y = 3x - 2 \\ y = -x - 6 \end{cases}$

3. $(3, 14)$; $\begin{cases} x = \frac{1}{2}y - 4 \\ y = 4x + 2 \end{cases}$

Solve each system by graphing.

4. $\begin{cases} x - 2y = 3 \\ y + x = 0 \end{cases}$

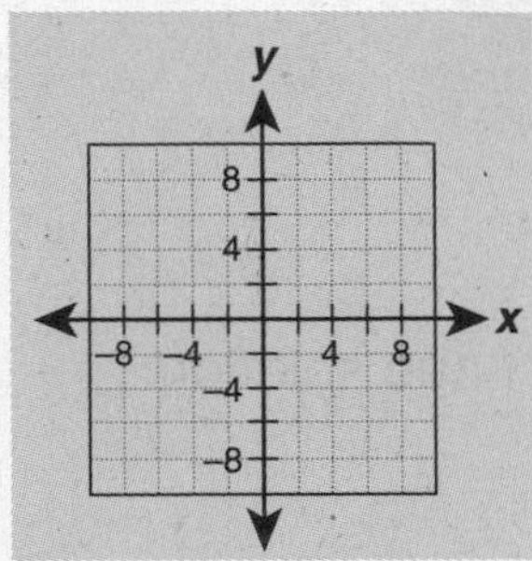

5. $\begin{cases} x = 6 - y \\ 2 - x = -y \end{cases}$

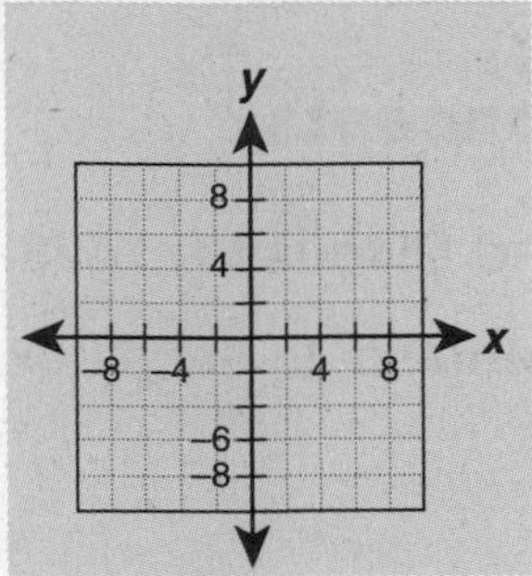

6-2 Solving Systems by Substitution

Solve each system by substitution.

6. $\begin{cases} x + 2y = 16 \\ x - 3y = 1 \end{cases}$

7. $\begin{cases} 7x + 5y = 175 \\ x + y = 23 \end{cases}$

8. $\begin{cases} 2x + y = -9 \\ 3x + 4y = -11 \end{cases}$

9. The sum of two numbers is 66. The second number is 22 less than three times the first number. Write and solve a system of equations to find the two numbers.

6-3 Solving Systems by Elimination

Solve each system by elimination.

10. $\begin{cases} 4y = 25 - 3x \\ 4x = 7y - 16 \end{cases}$

11. $\begin{cases} 3x - y = -137 \\ y = 2x + 99 \end{cases}$

12. $\begin{cases} 2x + y = -21 \\ 12x - 13y = 387 \end{cases}$

13. John needs 23 boards to build rafters for his house. He can use 16-foot or 20-foot length boards. He needs seven fewer 16-foot boards than 20-foot boards. Write and solve a system of equations to determine how many of each size board John needs.

6-4 Solving Special Systems

Solve each system of linear equations.

14. $\begin{cases} 4y - 6x = 10 \\ 15 + 9x = 6y \end{cases}$

15. $\begin{cases} 2x - 5y = 15 \\ 10y = 20 + 4x \end{cases}$

16. $\begin{cases} 6x + 14y = 16 \\ 24 - 9x = 21y \end{cases}$

Classify each system. Give the number of solutions.

17. $\begin{cases} y - 3x = 3 \\ 3(x - 1) = y \end{cases}$

18. $\begin{cases} y + x = 3 \\ 6 = 2x - y \end{cases}$

19. $\begin{cases} 3x = -y - 2 \\ 2y + 4 = -6x \end{cases}$

6-5 Solving Linear Inequalities

Tell whether the ordered pair is a solution of the inequality.

20. $(-4, 2)$; $y \geq 2x - 4$ **21.** $(6, 8)$; $y < 2x - 4$ **22.** $(1, 2)$; $2y \leq x + 3$

Graph the solutions of each linear inequality.

23. $y \geq 2x - 2$

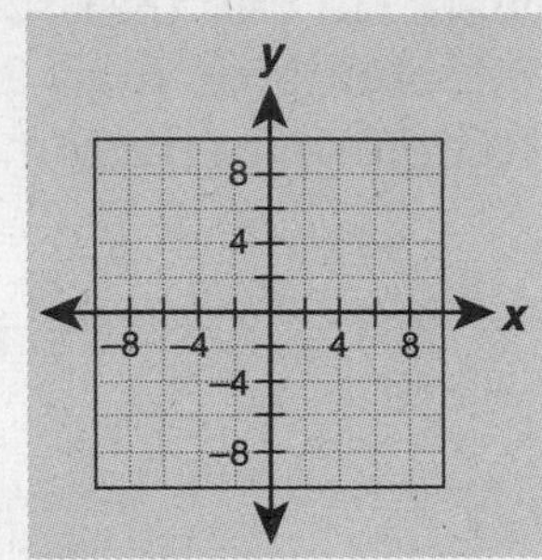

24. $y + \frac{1}{2}x \leq 1$

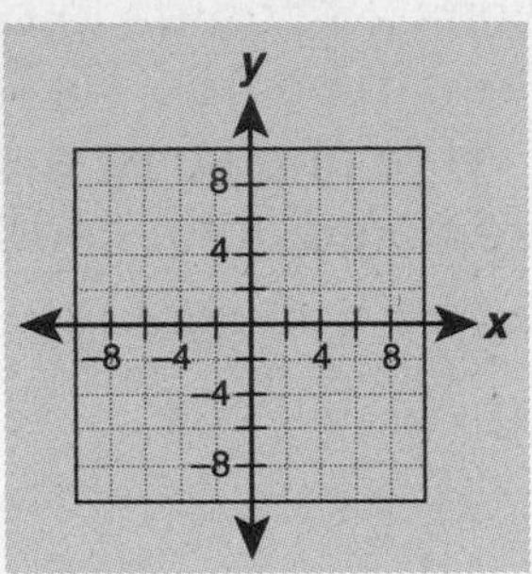

6-6 Solving Systems of Linear Inequalities

Tell whether the ordered pair is a solution of the given system.

25. $(0, 0)$; $\begin{cases} x + 2y < 4 \\ 2y > x - 6 \end{cases}$ **26.** $(-2, 2)$; $\begin{cases} y \geq x + 3 \\ 2x \geq 3y + 2 \end{cases}$ **27.** $(4, -3)$; $\begin{cases} 2y - x < -6 \\ 2x \geq -3y \end{cases}$

Graph each system of linear inequalities.

28. $\begin{cases} 2x - y > -3 \\ 4x + y < 5 \end{cases}$

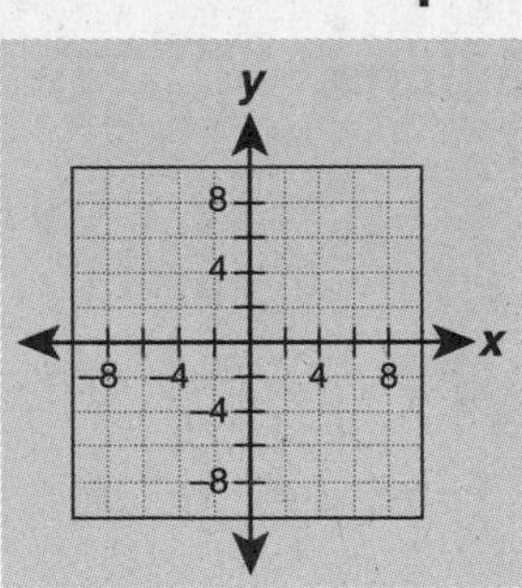

29. $\begin{cases} x - y < -2 \\ x - y > 2 \end{cases}$

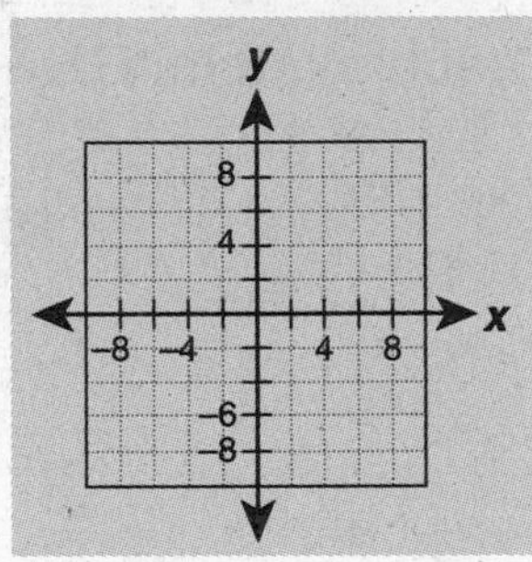

Big Ideas

Answer these questions to summarize the important concepts from Chapter 6 in your own words.

1. What are the steps for solving systems of equations by using substitution?

2. Explain which method is best for solving systems of linear equations for certain systems.

3. What are the steps for graphing inequalities?

4. Explain what the graph of a dependent, consistent, and inconsistent system looks like.

For more review of Chapter 6:

- Complete the Chapter 6 Study Guide and Review on pages 430–433.
- Compete the Ready to Go On quizzes on pages 413 and 429.

Vocabulary

This table contains important vocabulary terms from Chapter 7. As you work through the chapter, fill in the page number, definition, and a clarifying example for each term.

Term	Page	Definition	Clarifying Example
binomial			
cubic			
degree of a monomial			
degree of a polynomial			
difference of two squares			
leading coefficient			
monomial			
perfect-square trinomial			
polynomial			
quadratic			
scientific notation			

Term	Page	Definition	Clarifying Example
standard form of a polynomial			
trinomial			

Integer Exponents

Lesson Objectives

Evaluate expressions containing zero and integer exponents; Simplify expressions containing zero and integer exponents

Key Concepts

Integer Exponents (p. 446):

WORDS	NUMBERS	ALGEBRA

Think and Discuss (p. 448)

Get Organized In each box, describe how to simplify, and give an example.

Simplifying Expressions with Negative Exponents

For a negative exponent in the numerator . . .	For a negative exponent in the denominator . . .

LESSON **7-2**

Powers of 10 and Scientific Notation

Lesson Objectives

Evaluate and multiply by powers of 10; Convert between standard notation and scientific notation

Vocabulary

scientific notation (p. 453) ____________________

____

Key Concepts

Powers of 10 (p. 452):

WORDS	NUMBERS
Positive Integer Exponent	
Negative Integer Exponent	

Multiplying by Powers of 10 (p. 453):

Think and Discuss (p. 454)

Get Organized Complete the graphic organizer.

Powers of 10 and Scientific Notation

A negative exponent corresponds to moving the decimal point ______.

A positive exponent corresponds to moving the decimal point ______.

LESSON 7-3

Multiplication Properties of Exponents

Lesson Objectives

Use multiplication properties of exponents to evaluate and simplify expressions

Key Concepts

Simplifying Exponential Expressions (p. 460):

Simplifying Exponential Expressions	
An exponential expression is completely simplified if . . .	
Examples	Nonexamples

Product of Powers Property (p. 460):

WORDS	NUMBERS	ALGEBRA

Power of a Power Property (p. 462):

WORDS	NUMBERS	ALGEBRA

Power of a Product Property (p. 463):

WORDS	NUMBERS	ALGEBRA

Think and Discuss (p. 463)

Get Organized In each box, supply the missing exponents. Then give an example for each property.

Multiplication Properties of Exponents		
Product of Powers Property	Power of a Power Property	Power of a Product Property

LESSON 7-4

Division Properties of Exponents

Lesson Objectives

Use division properties of exponents to evaluate and simplify expressions

Key Concepts

Quotient of Powers Property (p. 467):

WORDS	NUMBERS	ALGEBRA

Positive Power of a Quotient Property (p. 469):

WORDS	NUMBERS	ALGEBRA

Negative Power of a Quotient Property (p. 470):

WORDS	NUMBERS	ALGEBRA

Think and Discuss (p. 471)

Get Organized In each box, write an equation that has the indicated number of solutions.

If *a* and *b* are nonzero real numbers and *m* and *n* are integers, then...		
$\frac{a^m}{a^n} =$	$\left(\frac{a}{b}\right)^n =$	$\left(\frac{a}{b}\right)^{-n} =$

LESSON 7-5

Polynomials

Lesson Objectives

Classify polynomials and write polynomials in standard form; Evaluate polynomial expressions

Vocabulary

monomial (p. 476) ______________________________

____

degree of a monomial (p. 476) ______________________________

____

polynomial (p. 476) ______________________________

____

degree of a polynomial (p. 476) ______________________________

____

standard form of a polynomial (p. 477) ______________________________

____

leading coefficient (p. 477) ______________________________

____

quadratic (p. 476) ______________________________

____

cubic (p. 476) ______________________________

____

binomial (p. 476) ______________________________

____

trinomial (p. 476) ______________________________

____

Key Concepts

Think and Discuss (p. 478)

Get Organized In each circle, write an example of the given type of polynomial.

LESSON 7-6

Adding and Subtracting Polynomials

Lesson Objectives

Add and subtract polynomials

Key Concepts

Think and Discuss (p. 486)

Get Organized In each box, write an example that shows how to perform the given operation.

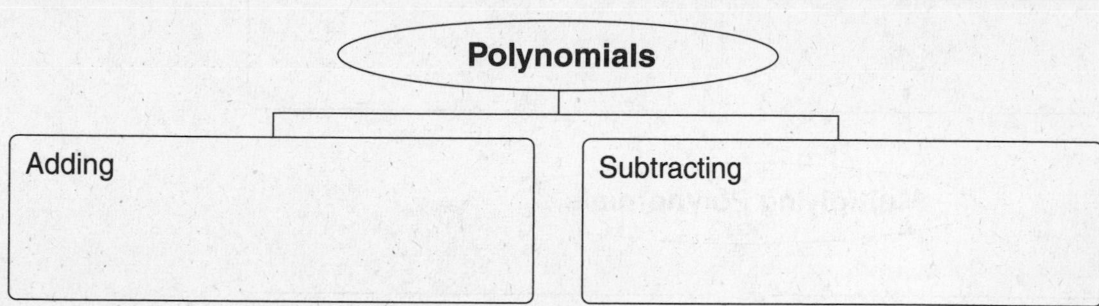

Multiplying Polynomials

Lesson Objectives

Multiply polynomials

Key Concepts

Think and Discuss (p. 496)

Get Organized In each box, multiply two polynomials using the given method.

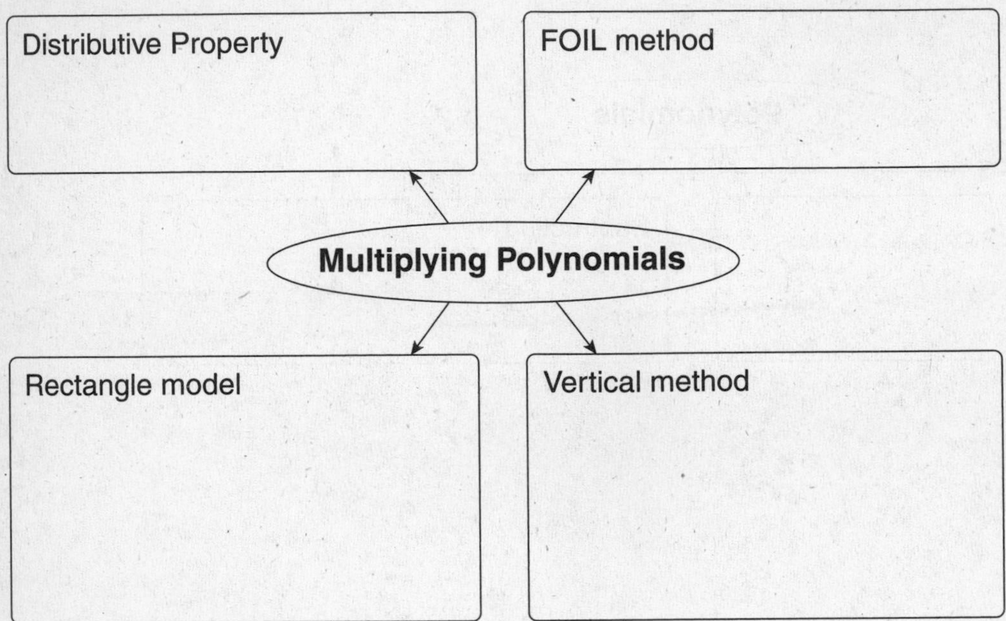

LESSON 7-8

Special Products of Binomials

Lesson Objectives

Find special products of binomials

Vocabulary

perfect-square trinomial (p. 501): ______________________________

____

difference of two squares (p. 503): ______________________________

____

Key Concepts

Special Products of Binomials (p. 504):

Special Products of Binomials

Think and Discuss (p. 505)

Get Organized Complete the special product rules and give an example of each.

Special Products of Binomials		
Perfect-Square Trinomials		Difference of Two Squares
$(a + b)^2 =$	$(a - b)^2 =$	$(a + b)(a - b) =$

CHAPTER 7

Chapter Review

7-1 Integer Exponents

Simplify.

1. $25g^0$
2. $s^{-2}r^3$
3. $\dfrac{3p^{-2}g^{-3}}{2t^0}$
4. $\frac{1}{3}x^{-2}y^4$

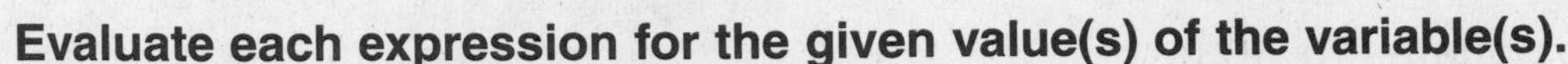

Evaluate each expression for the given value(s) of the variable(s).

5. $(b - 4)^{-3}$ for $b = 4$
6. x^2y^0 for $x = 3$ and $y = 6$
7. $(2mn)^{-2}m = 3$ and $n = -2$

7-2 Powers of 10 and Scientific Notation

8. Find the value of 10^{-6}.
9. Write 10,000,000 as a power of 10.
10. Find the value of 14.2×10^3
11. Write 0.0000001715 in scientific notation.
12. The average diameter of a human hair is 0.00006 meters. Write this number in scientific notation.

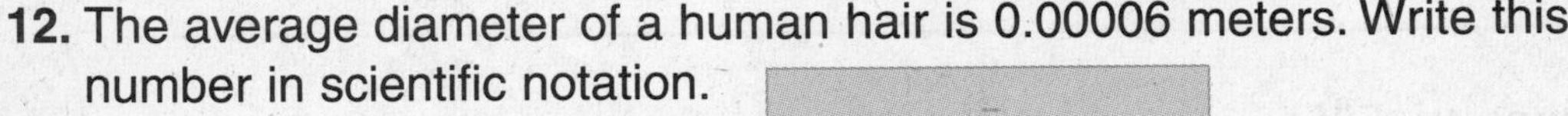

7-3 Multiplication Properties of Exponents

Simplify.

13. $4^4 \cdot 4^{-5} \cdot 4^3$

14. $x^{-2} \cdot x^3 \cdot y^5$

15. $(-2s^2t^3)^2$

16. $(m^2n)^4 \cdot (m^4n^3)^2$

17. $(2xy^2)^4 \cdot (x^2y)^{-3}$

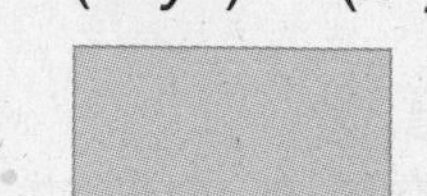

18. $-(r^2)^{-3} \cdot (-r^2)^3$

19. $(x^by^{2r})^3$

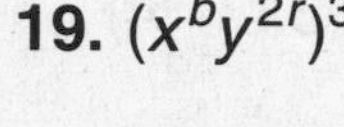

20. $(x + 2)^{-3} \cdot (x + 2)$

7-4 Division Properties of Exponents

Simplify.

21. $\frac{x^6}{x^3}$

22. $\left(\frac{4}{5}\right)^3$

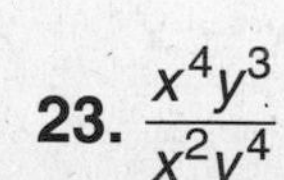

23. $\frac{x^4y^3}{x^2y^4}$

24. $\left(\frac{rs^4}{r^4s^2}\right)^{-2}$

25. In 1867, the United States purchased Alaska from Russia for $7.2 million. The total area of Alaska is about 3.78×10^8 acres. What was the price per acre? Write your answer in standard form.

7-5 Polynomials

Write each polynomial in standard form and give the leading coefficient.

26. $-4x^2 - x^3 + 3$

27. $15y - 6 + 10y^3 - 3y^2$

Classify each polynomial according to its degree and number of terms.

28. $6x + 3x^2 + 1$

29. $16 - 4x^3 + 3x^2$

7-6 Adding and Subtracting Polynomials

Add or subtract.

30. $(-3y + 2) + (y^2 + 3y + 2)$

31. $(2x^2 + 3x - 4) - (x^2 + x - 1)$

32. $(-2x^3 - x + 8) - (-2x^3 + 3x - 4)$

33. $(-4x^3 - 2x^2 + x - 5) + (2x^3 + 3x + 4)$

7-7 Multiplying Polynomials

Multiply.

34. $(3x - 7)(-2x)$

35. $3x^2(5x - x^3 + 2)$

36. $(3x - 2)(5x + 7)$

37. $(x - 5)(2x + 10)$

38. $(x^2 + 9)(x^2 - x - 4)$

39. $(2x^2 - 7x + 1)(4x + 3)$

7-8 Special Products of Binomials

Multiply.

40. $(2x + 1)^2$

41. $(2 + 3y)^2$

42. $(3y - 2)^2$

43. $(4x + 3y)^2$

44. $(5x - 6)(5x + 6)$

45. $(4x - 7y)(4x + 7y)$

46. The height traveled (in feet) of a bottle rocket is modeled by $h = -16t^2 + 57t$ where t is the time in seconds. Find the height of the rocket after 2 seconds.

CHAPTER 7

Big Ideas

Answer these questions to summarize the important concepts from Chapter 7 in your own words.

1. Explain why the properties using zero exponents and negative exponents specify that bases must be "nonzero numbers".

2. Explain the difference between multiplying by powers of 10 when the exponent is a positive number and when the exponent is a negative number.

3. When is an exponential expression completely simplified?

4. Explain how to multiply $(x + 3)(x + 2)$ using the FOIL method.

For more review of Chapter 7:

- Complete the Chapter 7 Study Guide and Review on pages 510–513.
- Compete the Ready to Go On quizzes on pages 475 and 509.

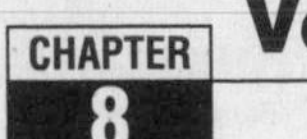

Vocabulary

This table contains important vocabulary terms from Chapter 8. As you work through the chapter, fill in the page number, definition, and a clarifying example for each term.

Term	Page	Definition	Clarifying Example
greatest common factor			

Term	Page	Definition	Clarifying Example
prime factorization			

LESSON 8-1

Factors and Greatest Common Factors

Lesson Objectives

Write the prime factorization of numbers, find the GCF of monomials

Vocabulary

prime factorization (p. 524): ______________________________

____

greatest common factor (p. 525): ______________________________

____

Key Concepts

Think and Discuss (p. 526)

Get Organized In each box, write an example of an equation that can be solved by using the given property, and solve it.

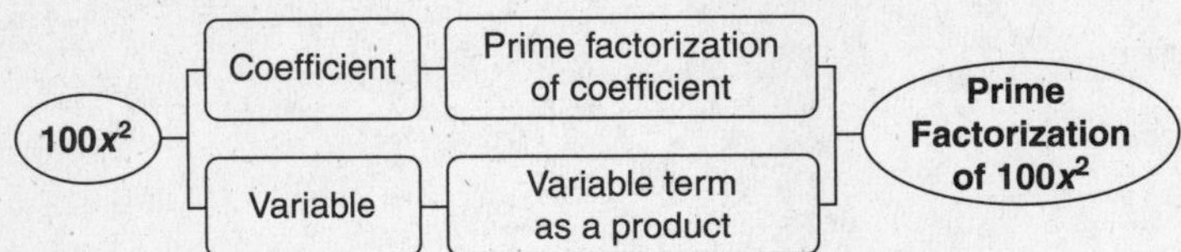

LESSON 8-2

Factoring by GCF

Know it!
Note

Lesson Objectives

Factor polynomials by using the greatest common factor

Key Concepts

Think and Discuss (p. 534)

Get Organized Complete the graphic organizer.

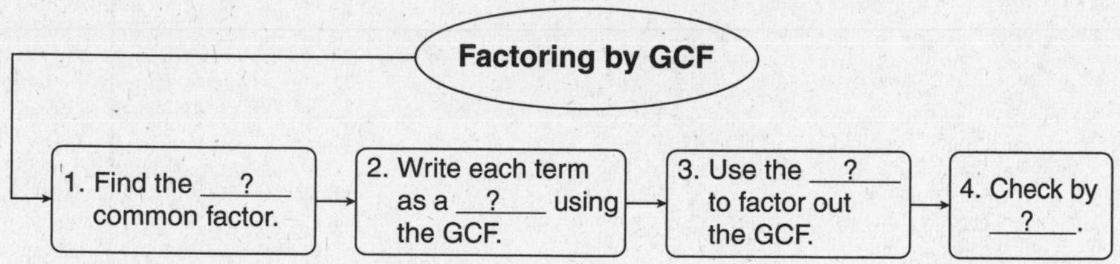
Factoring by GCF
1. Find the ___?___ common factor.
2. Write each term as a ___?___ using the GCF.
3. Use the ___?___ to factor out the GCF.
4. Check by ___?___.

LESSON 8-3

Factoring $x^2 + bx + c$

Lesson Objectives

Factor quadratic trinomials of the form $x^2 + bx + c$

Key Concepts

Factoring $x^2 + bx + c$ (p. 541):

WORDS	EXAMPLE

Think and Discuss (p. 543)

Get Organized In each box, write an example of a trinomial with the given properties and factor it.

Factoring
$x^2 + bx + c$

c is positive, and b is positive.

c is negative, and b is positive.

c is positive, and b is negative.

c is negative, and b is negative.

LESSON 8-4

Factoring $ax^2 + bx + c$

Lesson Objectives

Factor quadratic trinomials of the form $ax^2 + bx + c$

Key Concepts

Think and Discuss (p. 551)

Get Organized In each box, write an equation that has the indicated number of solutions.

Factoring $ax^2 + bx + c$	
$c > 0$	
$b > 0$	$b < 0$
$c < 0$	
$b < 0$	$b > 0$

LESSON **8-5**

Factoring Special Products

Lesson Objectives

Factor perfect-square trinomials; Factor the difference of two squares

Key Concepts

Perfect-Square Trinomials (p. 558):

PERFECT-SQUARE TRINOMIAL	EXAMPLES

Difference of Two Squares (p. 560):

DIFFERENCE OF TWO SQUARES	EXAMPLE

Think and Discuss (p. 561)

Get Organized Write an example of each type of special product and factor it.

Special Product	Factored Form
Perfect-square trinomial with positive coefficient of middle term	
Perfect-square trinomial with negative coefficient of middle term	
Difference of two squares	

LESSON 8-6

Choosing a Factoring Method

Lesson Objectives

Choose an appropriate method for factoring a polynomial; Combine methods for factoring a polynomial

Key Concepts

Methods to Factor Polynomials (p. 568):

METHODS TO FACTOR POLYNOMIALS	
Any Polynomial	
Binomials	
Trinomials	
Polynomials of Four or More Terms	

Think and Discuss (p. 568)

Get Organized Draw an arrow from each expression to the method you would use to factor it.

Factoring Methods	
Polynomial	**Method**
1. $16x^4 - 25y^8$	**A.** Factoring out the GCF
2. $x^2 + 10x + 25$	**B.** Factoring by grouping
3. $9t^2 + 27t + 18t^4$	**C.** Unfactorable
4. $a^2 + 3a - 7a - 21$	**D.** Difference of two squares
5. $100b^2 + 81$	**E.** Perfect-square trinomial

Chapter Review

8-1 Factors and Greatest Common Factors

Write the prime factorization of each number.

1. 66

2. 72

3. 325

4. 169

Find the GCF of each pair of monomials.

5. $30r^4$ and $12r^3$

6. $24z^3$ and $32z^2$

7. $16x^2y$ and $84xy^2$

8. $99s^6t^3$ and $45s^3t^6$

8-2 Factoring by GCF

Factor each polynomial. Check your answer.

9. $2s^2 - 4$

10. $-a^3 - 4a$

11. $36y^4 + 24y^2$

12. $4x^2 - 8x + 8$

13. $3b^3 - 15b^2 - 33b$

14. $14p^3 - 21p^2q$

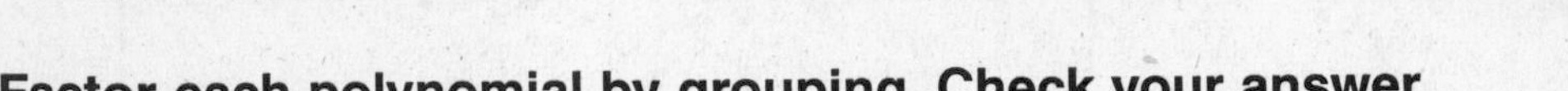

Factor each polynomial by grouping. Check your answer.

15. $r^3 + 3r^2 + 2r + 6$

16. $7y^3 - 14y^2 - y + 2$

17. $5x^3 + 10x^2 + 3x + 6$

8-3 Factoring $x^2 + bx + c$

Factor each trinomial. Check your answer.

18. $a^2 - 5a - 14$

19. $x^2 + 7x + 10$

20. $n^2 + 4n - 12$

21. $f^2 - 11f + 18$ **22.** $z^2 - z - 20$ **23.** $t^2 - t - 30$

24. Factor $x^2 - 7x + 12$. Check your answer.

8-4 Factoring $ax^2 + bx + c$

Factor each trinomial. Check your answer.

25. $3a^2 + 5a + 2$ **26.** $6s^2 + 17s + 12$ **27.** $5y^2 - 18y - 8$

28. $10z^2 + 12z - 16$ **29.** $21x^2 + 44x - 32$ **30.** $6t^2 - 31t + 35$

31. The area of a rectangle is $5x^2 + 22x + 8$ cm^2. The width is $(x + 4)$ cm.

What is the length of the rectangle?

8-5 Factoring Special Products

Determine whether each trinomial is a perfect square. If so, factor it.

32. $9t^2 - 30t + 25$ **33.** $z^2 + 8z - 16$ **34.** $4y^2 + 36y + 81$

35. $4x^2 - 28x + 49$ **36.** $b^2 - 16b + 64$ **37.** $16m^2 + 12m + 9$

Determine whether each trinomial is the difference of two squares. If so, factor it.

38. $1 - 10s^4$

39. $t^2 - 9$

40. $121x^2 - 100$

41. $25h^2 - 20$

42. $9z^4 + 25$

43. $25y^4 - 16x^2$

8-6 Choosing a Factoring Method

Factor each polynomial completely. Check your answer.

44. $25b^3 + 30b^2 - 60b$

45. $2x^2y + 16xy + 30y$

46. $c^3 - 6c^2 - 4c + 24$

Write an expression for the situation. Factor your expression.

47. Nine times the square of Teresa's shoe size plus twelve times Teresa's shoe size plus four

48. The difference of the square of four times a DVD cost and 49

Big Ideas

Answer these questions to summarize the important concepts from Chapter 8 in your own words.

1. Explain how to find the GCF of two terms that contain the same variable raised to different exponents.

2. What are the steps for factoring the GCF?

3. Explain, in words, how to factor the quadratic trinomial $x^2 + bx + c$.

4. Explain how to determine the signs of the factors of c when factoring a trinomial of the form $x^2 + bx + c$.

For more review of Chapter 8:

- Complete the Chapter 8 Study Guide and Review on pages 574–577 of your textbook.
- Compete the Ready to Go On quizzes on pages 557 and 573 of your textbook.

Vocabulary

This table contains important vocabulary terms from Chapter 9. As you work through the chapter, fill in the page number, definition, and a clarifying example for each term.

Term	Page	Definition	Clarifying Example
axis of symmetry			
completing the square			
discriminant			
maximum			
minimum			
parabola			

Term	Page	Definition	Clarifying Example
quadratic equation			
quadratic function			
vertex			
zero of a function			

Identifying Quadratic Functions

Lesson Objectives

Identify quadratic functions and determine whether they have a minimum or maximum; Graph a quadratic function and give its domain and range

Vocabulary

quadratic function (p. 590): ______________________

____

parabola (p. 591): ______________________

____

vertex (p. 592): ______________________

____

minimum (p. 592): ______________________

____

maximum (p. 592): ______________________

____

Key Concepts

Minimum and Maximum Values (p. 592):

WORDS		
GRAPHS		

Think and Discuss (p. 593)

Get Organized In each box, describe a way of identifying quadratic functions.

Identifying Quadratic Functions

LESSON 9-2

Characteristics of Quadratic Functions

Lesson Objectives

Find the zeros of a quadratic function from its graph; Find the axis of symmetry and the vertex of a parabola

Vocabulary

zero of a function (p. 599): ______________________________

____

axis of symmetry (p. 600): ______________________________

____

Key Concepts

Finding the Axis of Symmetry by Using Zeros (p. 600):

WORDS	NUMBERS	GRAPH
One Zero		4, 2, x, 0, (, 0), 4
Two Zeros		(, 0), 2, x, –4, –2, 0, –2, –4

Finding the Axis of Symmetry by Using the Formula (p. 601):

FORMULA	EXAMPLE

Finding the Vertex of a Parabola (p. 601):

FINDING THE VERTEX OF A PARABOLA
Step 1
Step 2
Step 3

Think and Discuss (p. 603)

Get Organized In each box, sketch a graph that fits the given description.

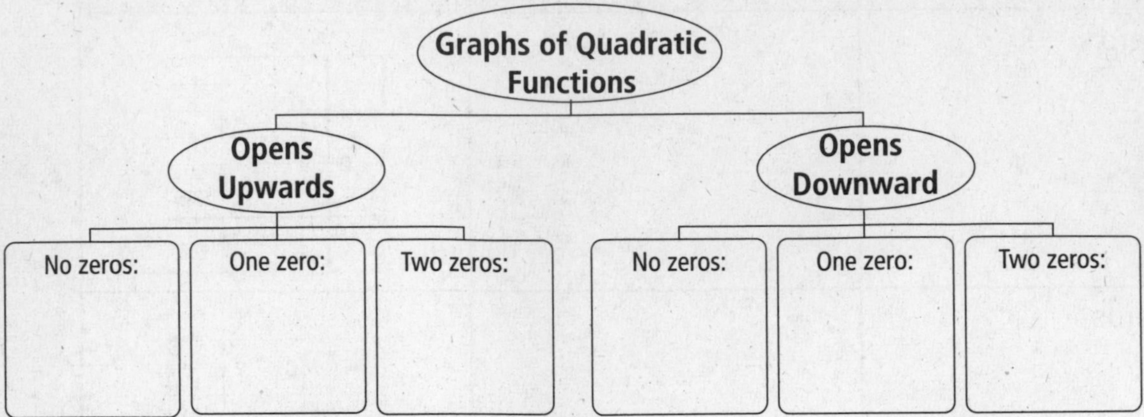

LESSON 9-3

Graphing Quadratic Functions

Lesson Objectives

Graph a quadratic function in the form $y = ax^2 + bx + c$

Key Concepts

Think and Discuss (p. 609)

Get Organized Complete the graphic organizer using your own quadratic function.

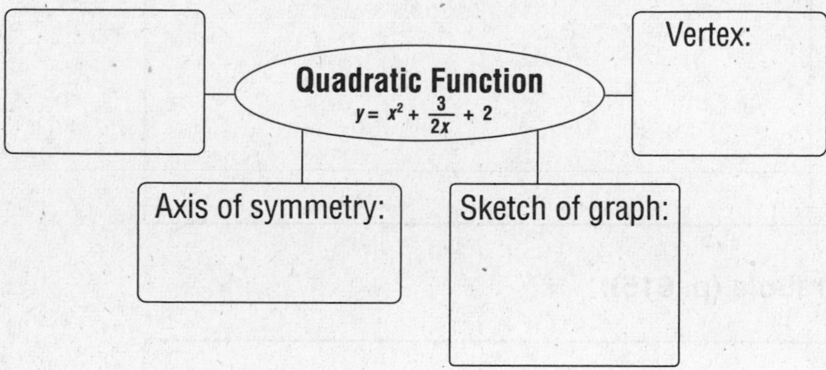

LESSON 9-4

Transforming Quadratic Functions

Lesson Objectives

Graph and transform quadratic functions

Key Concepts

Width of a Parabola (p. 613):

WORDS	EXAMPLES

Vertical Translations of a Parabola (p. 615):

Think and Discuss (p. 616)

Get Organized Complete the graphic organizer by explaining how each change affects the graph $y = ax^2 + c$.

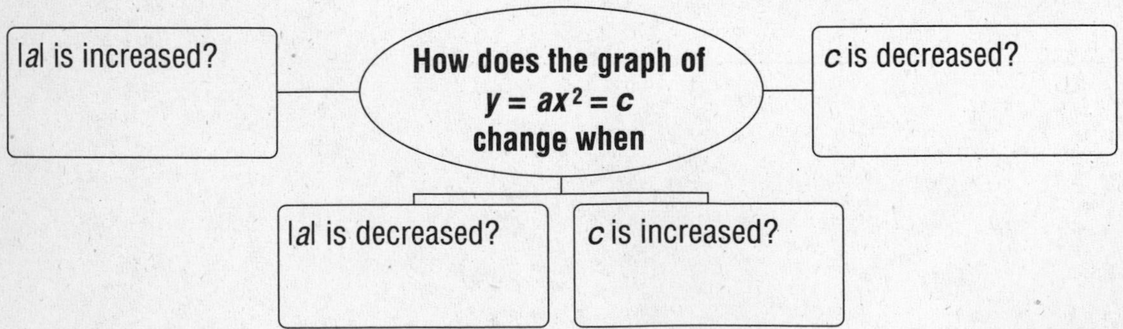

LESSON **9-5**

Solving Quadratic Equations by Graphing

Lesson Objectives

Solve quadratic equations by graphing

Vocabulary

quadratic equation (p. 622):) ______________________________

____

Key Concepts

Solving Quadratic Equations by Graphing (p. 622):

Step 1
Step 2
Step 3

Think and Discuss (p. 624)

Get Organized In each of the boxes, write the steps for solving quadratic equations by graphing.

Solving a Quadratic Equation by Graphing

1.

2.

3.

LESSON 9-6

Solving Quadratic Equations by Factoring

Lesson Objectives

Solve quadratic equations by factoring

Key Concepts

Zero Product Property (p. 630):

For all real numbers *a* and *b*,		
WORDS	**NUMBERS**	**ALGEBRA**

Think and Discuss (p. 633)

Get Organized In each box, write a step used to solve a quadratic equation by factory.

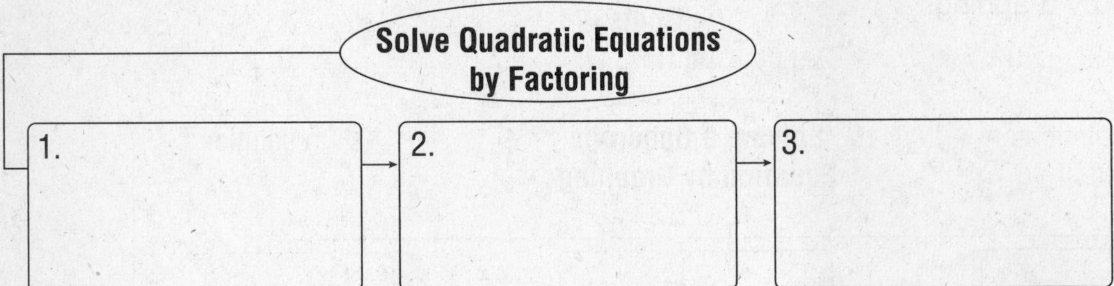

LESSON 9-7

Solving Quadratic Equations by Using Square Roots

Lesson Objectives

Solve quadratic equations by using square roots

Key Concepts

Square-Root Property (p. 636):

WORDS	NUMBERS	ALGEBRA

Think and Discuss (p. 639)

Get Organized In each box, write an example of a quadratic equation with the given number of solutions. Solve each equation.

Solving Quadratic Equations by Using Square Roots When the Equation Has....

No real solutions:	One solution:	Two solutions:

LESSON **9-8**

Completing the Square

Lesson Objectives

Solve quadratic equations by completing the square

Vocabulary

completing the square (p. 645): ______________________________

____

Key Concepts

Completing the Square (p. 645):

WORDS	NUMBERS	ALGEBRA

Solving a Quadratic Equation by Completing the Square (p. 646):

Step 1	
Step 2	
Step 3	
Step 4	
Step 5	
Step 6	

Think and Discuss (p. 648)

Get Organized In each box, write and solve an example using the given type of quadratic equation.

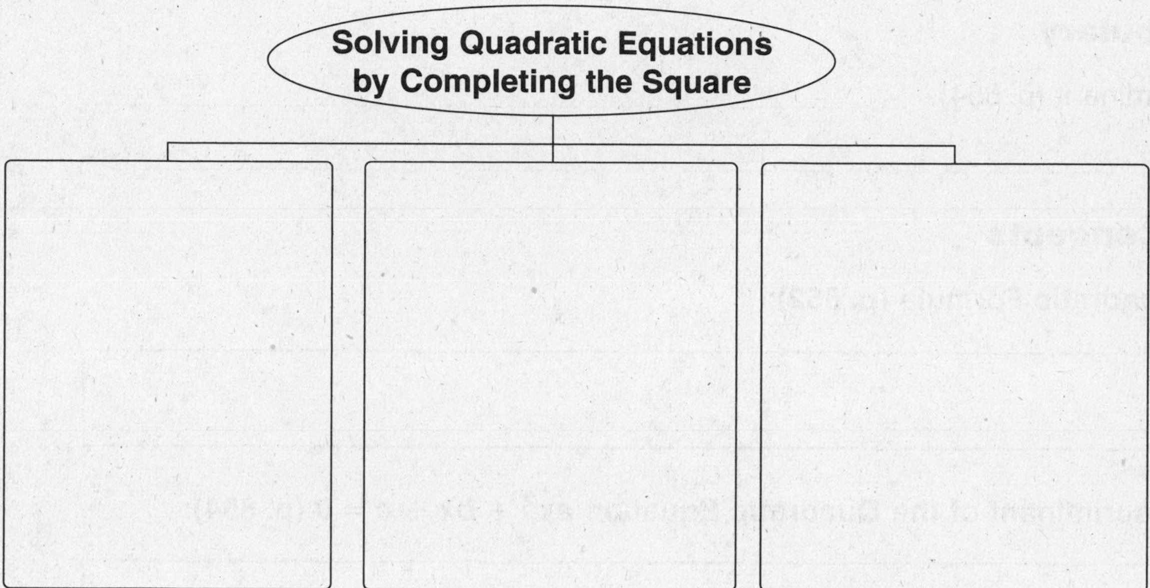

LESSON 9-9

The Quadratic Formula and the Discriminant

Lesson Objectives

Solve quadratic equations by using the Quadratic Formula; Determine the number of solutions of a quadratic equation by using the discriminant

Vocabulary

discriminant (p. 654): ______________________________

____

Key Concepts

The Quadratic Formula (p. 652):

The Discriminant of the Quadratic Equation $ax^2 + bx + c = 0$ (p. 654):

Method of Solving Quadratic Equations (p. 656):

METHOD	ADVANTAGES	DISADVANTAGES
Graphing		
Factoring		
Using square roots		
Completing the square		
Using the Quadratic Formula		

Think and Discuss (p. 657)

Get Organized In each box, write the number of real solutions.

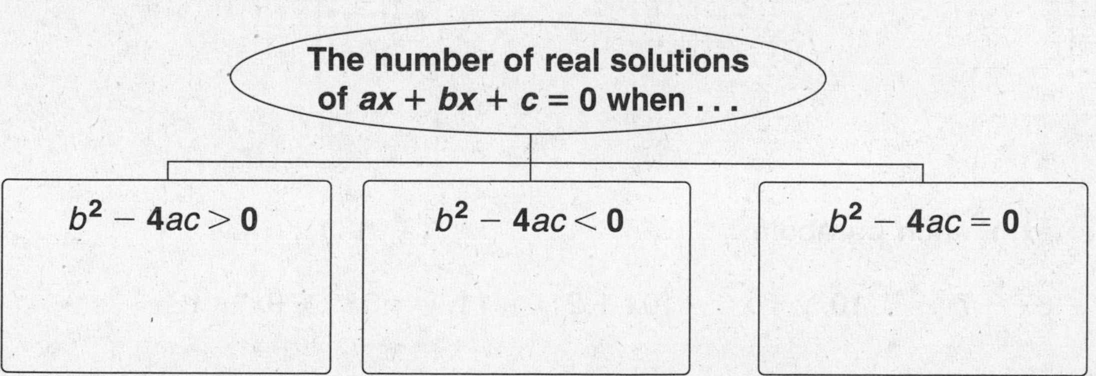

CHAPTER 9

Chapter Review

9-1 Identify Quadratic Functions

Tell whether each function is quadratic. Explain.

1. $y + 2 = 4x + 3x + 12$

2. $\{(-2, 11), (-1, 1), (0, -5), (1, -7), (2, -5)\}$

Tell whether the graph of each quadratic function opens upward or downward and whether the parabola has a maximum or a minimum.

3. $y = -x^2 + 4x - 1$

4. $y = 2x^2 + 3x + 5$

5. Graph the function $y = -\frac{3}{4}x^2 - x + 4$ and give the domain and range.

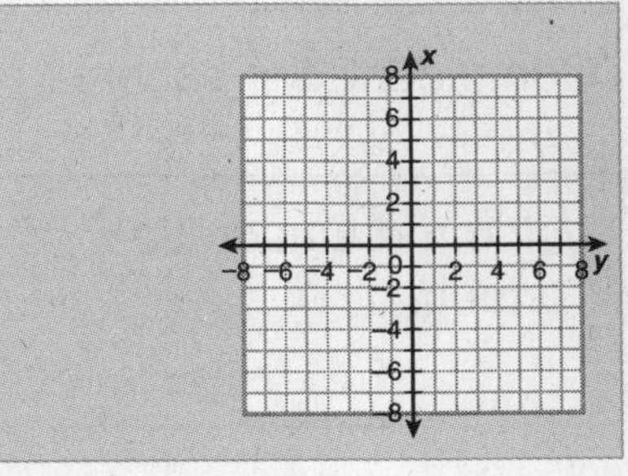

9-2 Characteristics of Quadratic Functions

Find the zeros of each function from its graph. Then find its axis of symmetry.

6.

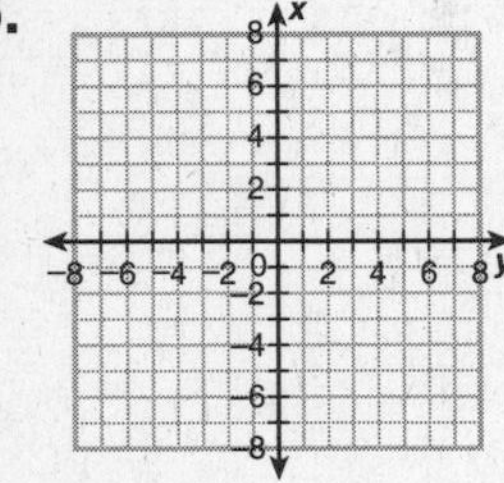

7.

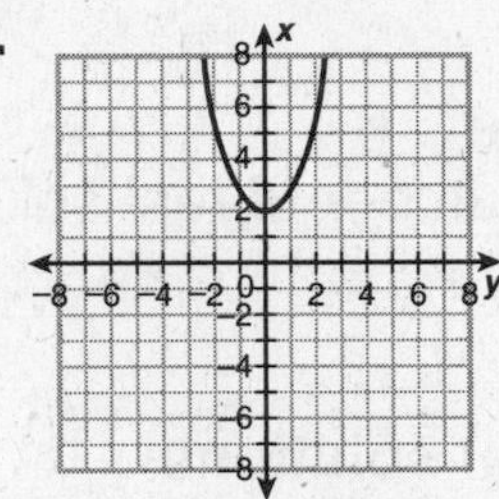

8.

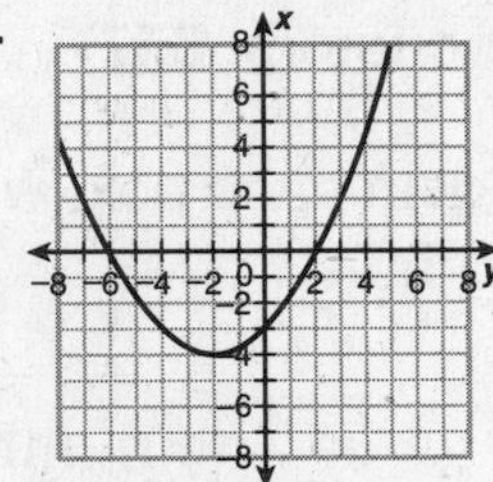

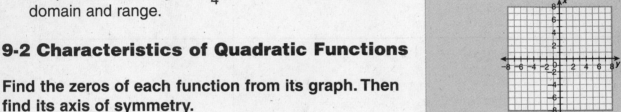

Find the vertex of each parabola.

9. $y = x^2 + 6x - 7$

10. $y = x^2 - 10x + 21$

11. $y = 3x^2 + 9x - 12$

9-3 Graphing Quadratic Functions

Graph each quadratic function.

12. $y = 2x^2 + 6x + 1$

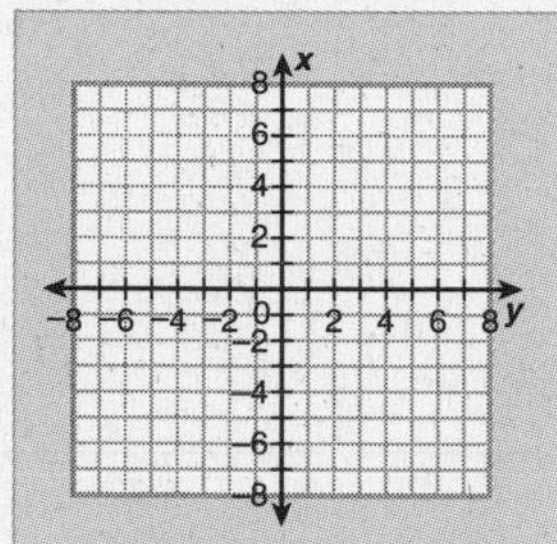

13. $y + 3x^2 = \frac{1}{3}x - 1$

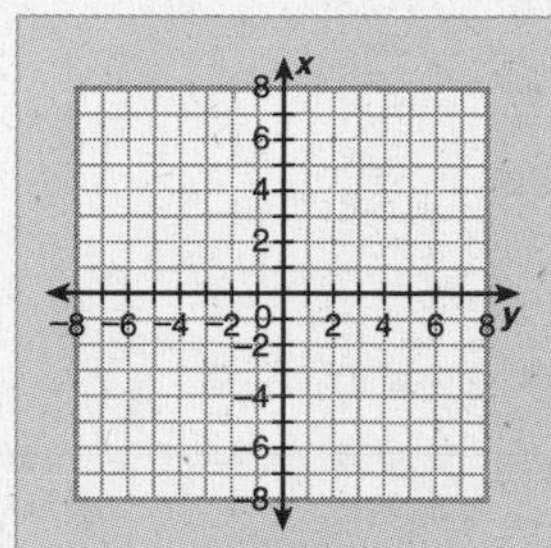

14. $y = \frac{1}{4}x^2 - 2x + 4$

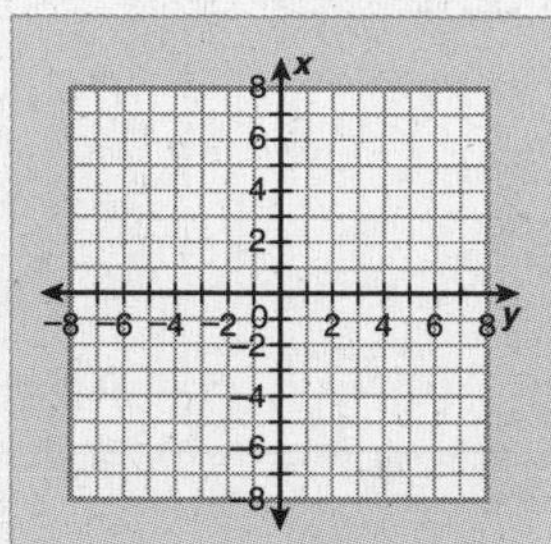

9-4 Transforming Quadratic Functions

Compare the graph of each function with the graph of $f(x) = x^2$.

15. $g(x) = x^2 - 5$

16. $g(x) = -\frac{4}{5}x^2$

9-5 Solving Quadratic Equations by Graphing

Solve each equation by graphing the related function.

17. $x^2 - 4x = 0$

18. $2x - 3 = -\frac{1}{3}x^2$

19. $-8x^2 - 4 = -16x$

20. A baseball is thrown upward with an initial velocity of 96 feet per second. The equation $h = -16t^2 + 96t$ represents the height, h, of a baseball after t seconds. Graph the equation. How long will it take the baseball to return to the ground?

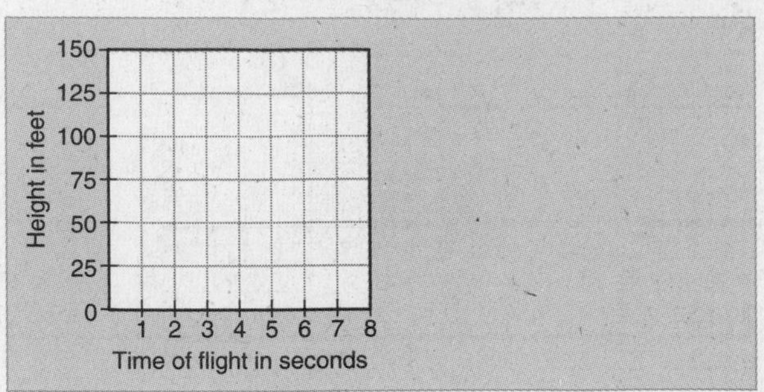

9-6 Solving Quadratic Equations by Factoring

Use the Zero Product Property to solve each equation.

21. $(x - 5)(x + 2) = 0$

22. $(2x - 5)(4x - 5) = 0$

23. $x(x - 5) = 0$

Solve each quadratic equation by factoring.

24. $x^2 + 5x + 6 = 0$

25. $2x^2 + 5x = 12$

26. $4x^2 = 4x - 1$

9-7 Solving Quadratic Equations by Using Square Roots

Solve using square roots.

27. $2x^2 = 72$

28. $0 = 5x^2 - 245$

29. $25x^2 - 16 = 0$

30. $4x^2 + 13 = 49$

31. $8x^2 + 10 = 42$

32. $36x^2 - 59 = -10$

Solve. Round to the nearest hundredth.

33. $84 - 7x^2 = -22$ **34.** $6x^2 + 44 = 128$ **35.** $13x^2 - 186 = 94$

9-8 Completing the Square

Complete the square for each expression.

36. $x^2 - 14x + ■$ **37.** $x^2 + 6x + ■$ **38.** $x^2 - 11x + ■$

Solve by completing the square.

39. $x^2 + 10x - 11 = 0$ **40.** $x^2 - 24x + 63 = 0$ **41.** $2x^2 - 6x = 20$

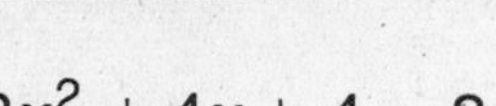

42. $3x^2 + 4x + 4 = 3$ **43.** $4x^2 - 12 = 0$ **44.** $x^2 - 2x = 2$

45. The area of a rectangle is given by $A = x^2 + 4x - 5$. Find the expressions for possible lengths and widths of the rectangle.

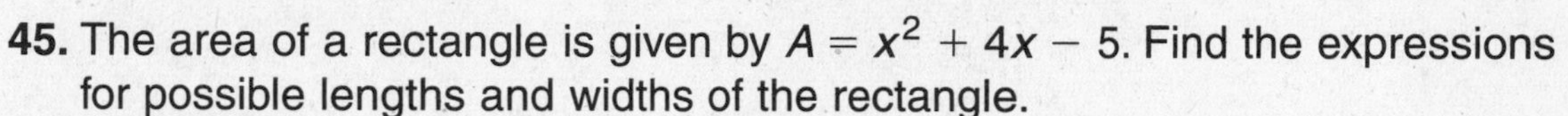

9-9 The Quadratic Formula and the Discriminant

Solve using the Quadratic Formula. Round your answer to the nearest hundredth.

46. $2x^2 - 4x - 3 = 0$ **47.** $4x^2 + 7x + 2 = 0$ **48.** $8x^2 + 10x - 33 = 0$

49. $x^2 + 2x = 1$ **50.** $2x^2 = 1 - 5x$ **51.** $x(x - 2) = 4$

Find the number of solutions of each equation using the discriminant.

52. $14x^2 - 19x - 40 = 0$

53. $10x^2 - 9x + 6 = 0$

54. $-3x^2 = 18x + 27$

55. $x^2 - 16x = -64$

56. $3x^2 = -2x - 5$

57. $2x^2 - 5x - 12 = 0$

Big Ideas

Answer these questions to summarize the important concepts from Chapter 9 in your own words.

1. Explain how to find the axis of symmetry of a parabola that opens upward or downward by using zeros.

2. Explain how to find the vertex of a parabola that opens upward or downward.

3. What are the steps of solving a quadratic equation by factoring?

4. What are the steps for solving a quadratic equation by completing the square?

For more review of Chapter 9:

- Complete the Chapter 9 Study Guide and Review on pages 662–665 of your textbook.
- Complete the Ready to Go On quizzes on pages 621 and 661 of your textbook.

Vocabulary

This table contains important vocabulary terms from Chapter 10. As you work through the chapter, fill in the page number, definition, and a clarifying example for each term.

Term	Page	Definition	Clarifying Example
bar graph			
box-and-whisker plot			
circle graph			
complement			
experiment			
histogram			

Term	Page	Definition	Clarifying Example
line graph			
mean			
median			
mode			
outcome			
outlier			
probability			
quartile			
range			
stem-and-leaf plot			

Organizing and Displaying Data

Lesson Objectives

Organize data in tables and graphs; choose a table or graph to display data

Vocabulary

bar graph (p. 678): ______________________________

line graph (p. 679): ______________________________

circle graph (p. 680): ______________________________

Key Concepts

Think and Discuss (p. 682)

Get Organized In each box, tell which kind of graph is described.

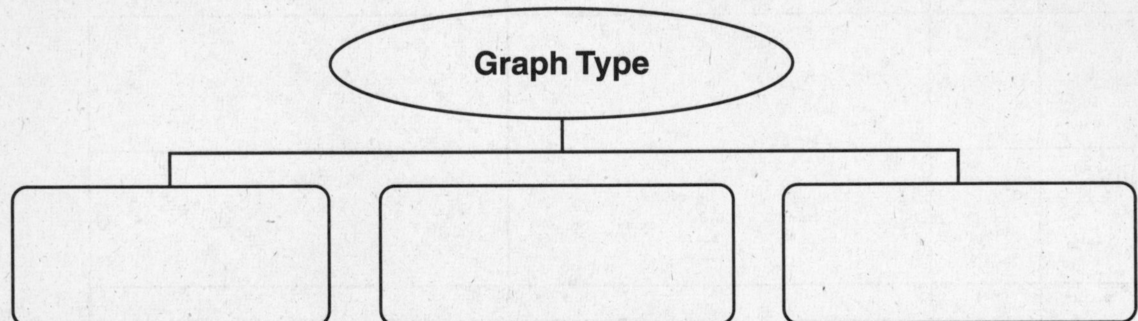

LESSON 10-2

Frequency and Histograms

Lesson Objectives

Create stem-and-leaf plots; Create frequency tables and histograms

Vocabulary

stem-and-leaf plot (p. 687): ______________________________

____

frequency (p. 688): ______________________________

____

frequency table (p. 688): ______________________________

____

histogram (p. 688): ______________________________

____

cumulative frequency (p. 689): ______________________________

____

Key Concepts

Think and Discuss (p. 689)

Get Organized Complete the graphic organizer.

Bar Graphs ↔ **Histograms**

How are they alike?	How are they different?

Data Distributions

Lesson Objectives

Describe the central tendency of a data set; Create box-and-whisker plots

Vocabulary

mean (p. 694): ______________________________

____

median (p. 694): ______________________________

____

mode (p. 694): ______________________________

____

range (p. 694): ______________________________

____

outlier (p. 695): ______________________________

____

quartile (p. 695): ______________________________

____

interquartile range (IQR) (p. 695): ______________________________

____

box-and-whisker plot (p. 695): ______________________________

____

Key Concepts

Think and Discuss (p. 696)

Get Organized Tell which measure of central tendency answers each question.

Measures of Central Tendency	
Measure	**Use to Answer**
	"What is the average?"
	"What is the halfway point of the data?"
	"What is the most common value?" (Can also be used to describe non-numerical data, such as favorite color.)

Misleading Graphs and Statistics

Lesson Objectives

Recognize misleading graphs; Recognize misleading statistics

Vocabulary

random sample (p. 703): ______________________________

____

Key Concepts

Think and Discuss (p. 703)

Get Organized Complete the graphic organizer. Add more boxes if needed.

Ways Graphs and Statistics can be Misleading

LESSON **10-5**

Experimental Probability

Lesson Objectives

Determine the experimental probability of an event; Use experimental probability to make predictions

Vocabulary

experiment (p. 713): ______________________________

trial (p. 713): ______________________________

outcome (p. 713): ______________________________

sample space (p. 713): ______________________________

event (p. 713): ______________________________

probability (p. 713): ______________________________

experimental probability (p. 714): ______________________________

prediction (p. 715): ______________________________

Key Concepts

Experimental Probability (p. 714):

Think and Discuss (p. 715)

Get Organized In each box, write an example of an event that has the given likelihood.

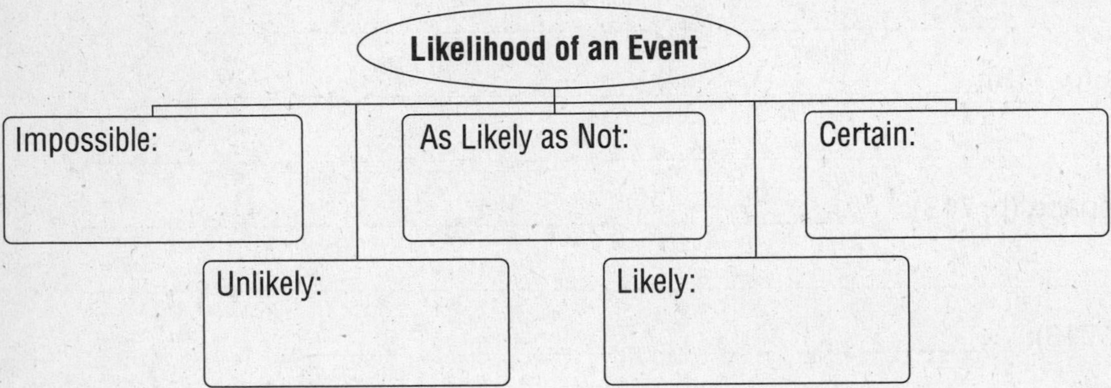

LESSON **10-6**

Theoretical Probability

Lesson Objectives

Determine the theoretical probability of an event; Convert between probabilities and odds

Vocabulary

equally likely (p. 720): ______________________________

____

theoretical probability (p. 720): ______________________________

____

fair (p. 720): ______________________________

____

complement (p. 721): ______________________________

____

odds (p. 722): ______________________________

____

Key Concepts

Theoretical Probability (p. 720):

$$\text{theoretical probability} = \frac{\text{number of ways the event can occur}}{\text{total number of equally likely outcomes}}$$

Odds (p. 722):

ODDS IN FAVOR OF AN EVENT
ODDS AGAINST AN EVENT

Think and Discuss (p. 723)

Get Organized Complete the graphic organizer using the spinner.

Probabilities on Spinner	
P(gray)	
P(not gray)	
Odds in favor of gray	
Odds against gray	

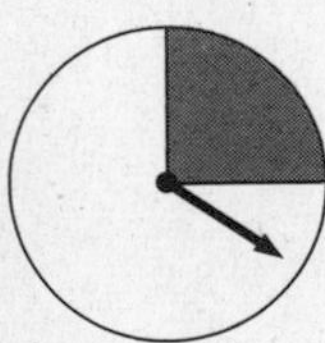

LESSON 10-7

Independent and Dependent Events

Lesson Objectives

Find the probability of independent events; Find the probability of dependent events

Vocabulary

independent events (p. 726): ______________________________

____

dependent events (p. 726): ______________________________

____

Key Concepts

Probability of Independent Events (p. 727):

Probability of Dependent Events (p. 729):

Think and Discuss (p. 730)

Get Organized Complete the graphic organizer.

Example of dependent events:	Example of independent events:

LESSON **10-8**

Combinations and Permutations

Lesson Objectives

solve problems involving permutations; solve problems involving combinations

Vocabulary

compound event (p. 737): ______________________________

____

combination (p. 737): ______________________________

____

permutation (p. 737): ______________________________

____

Key Concepts

Fundamental Counting Principle (p. 736):

If there are m ways to choose a first item and n ways to choose a second item after the first item has been chosen, then there are $m \cdot n$ ways to choose both items.

Permutations (p. 738):

FORMULA	
EXAMPLE	

Combinations (p. 739):

FORMULA	
EXAMPLE	

Think and Discuss (p. 739)

Get Organized Complete the graphic organizer.

	Fundamental Counting Principle	Permutation	Combination
When to use:			
Formula:			

CHAPTER 10

Chapter Review

10-1 Organizing and Displaying Data

1. The table shows fifty students' favorite colors. Choose a type of graph to display the given data. Make the graph, and explain why you chose that type of graph.

STUDENTS FAVORITE COLOR	
Number of Students	Color
6	blue
11	pink
17	red
10	yellow
6	green

10-2 Frequency and Histograms

2. Eleven tenth-grade classes had a car wash. The number of cars washed in a weekend is given below. Use the data to make a stem-and-leaf plot.

   15, 13, 9, 15, 30, 20, 26, 23, 23, 21, 18

3. The test scores of a science class are given below. Use the data to make a frequency table with intervals.

   73, 55, 82, 96, 76, 62, 43, 90, 68, 70, 85, 59, 66, 77, 81, 85, 65, 100, 61, 72, 42, 80, 75

10-3 Data Distributions

4. The average monthly rainfall in twelve consecutive months in one city was 73.6 mm, 62.6 mm, 90.5 mm, 95.6 mm, 117.5 mm, 95.8 mm, 113.2 mm, 100.5 mm, 82.8 mm, 72.3 mm, 94.4 mm, and 83.3 mm.

   a. Find the mean, median, mode, and range of the monthly rainfall.

b. Which value describes the average yearly rainfall?

c. Which value describes the spread of the data?

10-4 Misleading Graphs and Statistics

5. The graph shows how students divide a 24 hour day. Explain why the graph is misleading. What might people believe because of the graph? Who might want to use this graph?

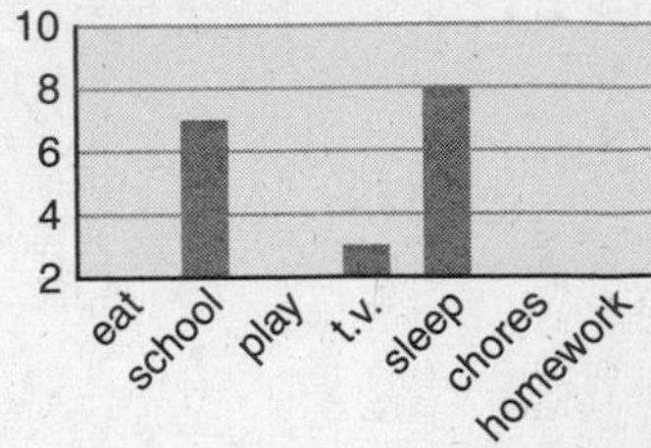

10-5 Experimental Probability

An experiment consists of pushing the random button on a MP3 player with seven different genres. Use the results in the table to find the experimental probability of each event.

Outcome	Frequency
Urban	9
Alternative	11
Rock	16
Classical	6
Country	11
Jazz	12
Reggae	5

6. selecting Reggae

7. selecting Urban and Classical

8. not selecting Jazz

9. selecting a genre that does not begin with the letter R

10. selecting a genre that begins with the letter C

10-6 Theoretical Probability

Find the theoretical probability of each outcome.

11. randomly choosing the letter E from the letters in TENNESSEE

12. flipping 3 coins and having all land heads up

13. The probability of winning a game is 40%. What are the odds of not winning?

14. rolling an even number on a number cube that is not a prime number

15. The odds against choosing a red marble from a bag are 2:9. What is the probability of choosing a red marble?

10-7 Independent and Dependant Events

16. A blue number cube and a yellow number cube are tossed. What is the probability that the number on the blue cube is even and the number on the yellow cube is less than 5?

17. Brian has a jar of quarters from 3 different states: 10 Ohio quarters, 15 Utah quarters and 25 Vermont quarters. Suppose Brian removes 3 quarters from the jar without replacing any of them. What is the probability that he will remove an Ohio quarter on the first draw, a Utah quarter on the second draw, and a Vermont quarter on the final draw?

18. A three-person endurance team is chosen randomly from a group of three men and three women. What is the probability that the team will consist of one women and one man?

10-8 Combinations and Permutations

19. There are 6 members of a club. How many ways can they elect a treasurer and a secretary?

20. How many ways can a sample of 4 chocolates be selected from a box of 12 chocolates?

21. Seven students are in the finals of a dance competition. Only first, second, and third place are awarded. How many ways can the students finish in the competition?

22. A standard deck of cards consists of 4 suits (spades, hearts, diamonds, and clubs) of 13 cards each. How many different ways can 5 cards be chosen from the deck?

23. How many different ways can 5 students line up in a row of 5?

24. A soccer team has 13 players. How many different ways can the coach choose two players to be captains?

Big Ideas

Answer these questions to summarize the important concepts from Chapter 10 in your own words.

1. Explain how to find the median when there is an even number of data values in a data set.

2. List four ways graphs and statistics can be misleading.

3. Explain the difference between experimental and theoretical probability.

4. Explain the difference between independent and dependent events. Give an example of an independent and a dependent event.

5. There are 15 players on the softball team. How many different ways can the coach choose 9 starters? Tell whether this situation involves combinations or permutations. Explain.

For more review of Chapter 10:

- Complete the Chapter 10 Study Guide and Review on pages 750–753.
- Complete the Ready to Go On quizzes on pages 711 and 745.

Vocabulary

This table contains important vocabulary terms from Chapter 11. As you work through the chapter, fill in the page number, definition, and a clarifying example for each term.

Term	Page	Definition	Clarifying Example
common ratio			
compound interest			
exponential decay			
exponential function			
exponential growth			
extraneous solution			
half-life			

Term	Page	Definition	Clarifying Example
geometric sequence			
like radicals			
radical equation			
radical expression			
radicand			
square root function			

Geometric Sequences

Lesson Objectives

Recognize and extend geometric sequences; Find the *n*th term of a geometric sequence

Vocabulary

geometric sequence (p. 766) ______________________________

____

common ratio (p. 766) ______________________________

____

Key Concepts

Think and Discuss (p. 768)

Get Organized In each box, write a way to represent the geometric sequence.

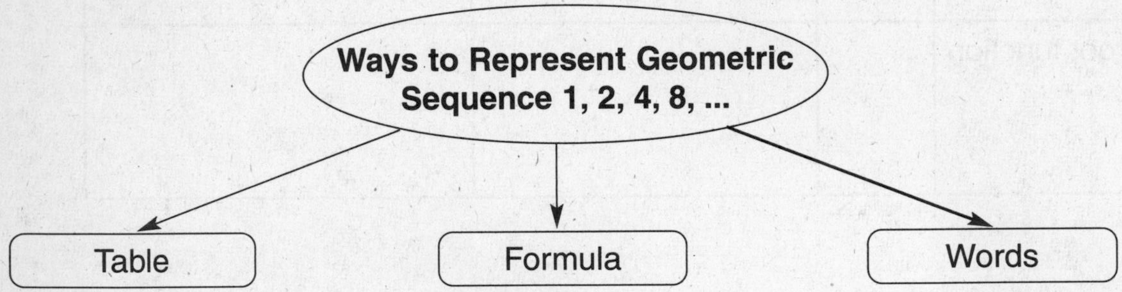

LESSON 11-2

Exponential Functions

Lesson Objectives

Evaluate exponential functions; Identify and graph exponential functions

Vocabulary

exponential function (p. 772) ______________________________

____

Key Concepts

Exponential Functions (p. 772):

Think and Discuss (p. 775)

Get Organized In each box, give an example of an appropriate exponential function and sketch its graph.

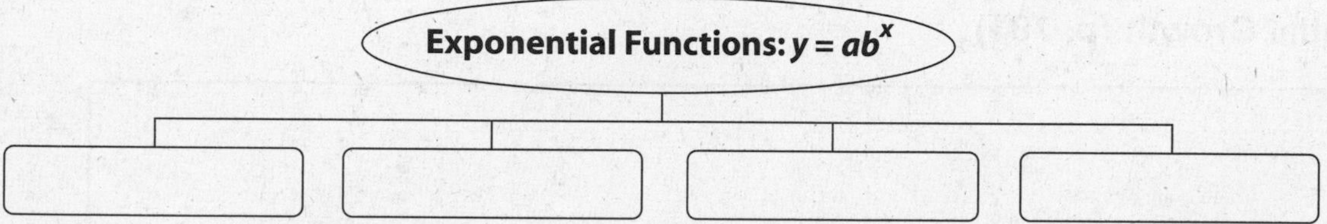

LESSON **11-3**

Exponential Growth and Decay

Lesson Objectives

Solve problems involving exponential growth and decay

Vocabulary

exponential growth (p. 781) ______________________________

____

compound interest (p. 782) ______________________________

____

exponential decay (p. 783) ______________________________

____

half-life (p. 783) ______________________________

____

Key Concepts

Exponential Growth (p. 781):

Compound Interest (p. 782):

Exponential Decay (p. 783):

Half-life (p. 783):

Think and Discuss (p. 784)

Get Organized Complete the graphic organizer.

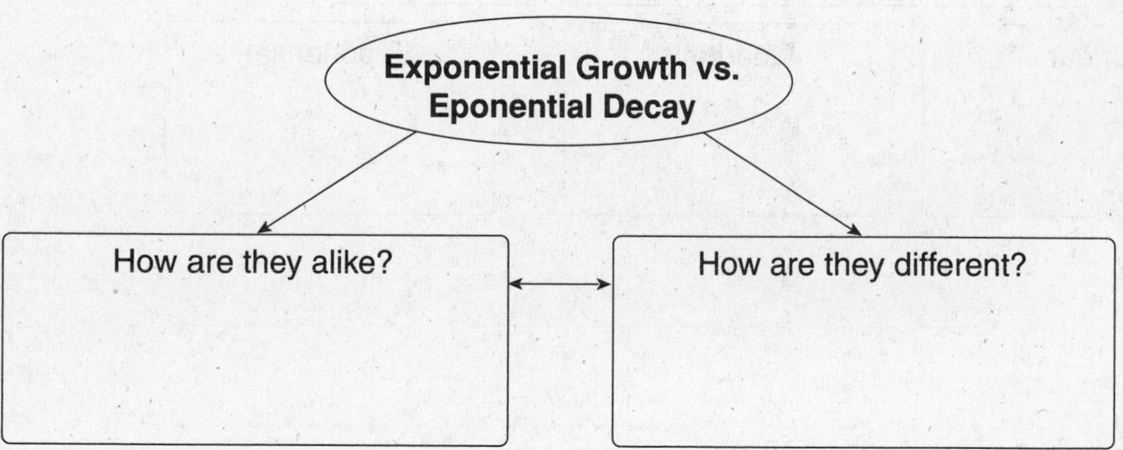
Exponential Growth vs. Eponential Decay
How are they alike?
How are they different?

LESSON 11-4

Linear, Quadratic, and Exponential Models

Lesson Objectives

Compare linear, quadratic, and exponential models; Given a set of data, decide which type of function models the data and write an equation to describe the function

Key Concepts

General Forms of Functions (p. 791):

LINEAR	QUADRATIC	EXPONENTIAL

Think and Discuss (p. 792)

Get Organized In each box, list some characteristics and sketch a graph of each type of model.

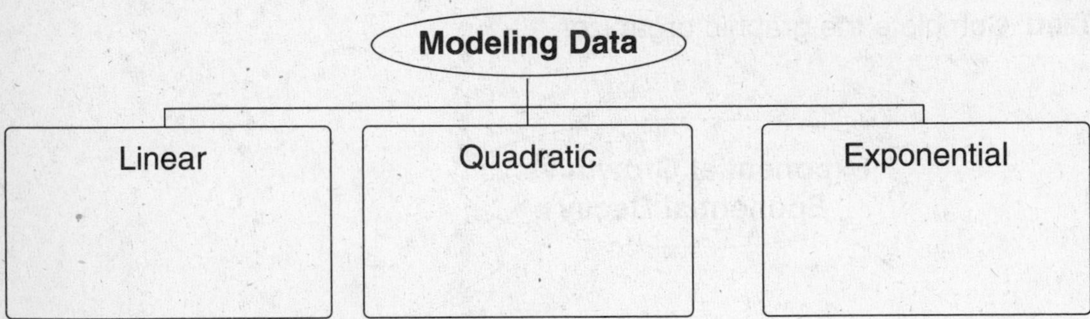

Square-Root Functions

Lesson Objectives

Identify square-root functions and their domains and ranges; Graph square-root functions

Vocabulary

square-root function (p. 798) ______________________________

____

Key Concepts

Square-Root Function (p. 798):

WORDS	EXAMPLES	NONEXAMPLES

Translation of the Graph of $f(x) = \sqrt{x}$ (p. 799):

Think and Discuss (p. 800)

Get Organized In each box, graph the function and give its domain.

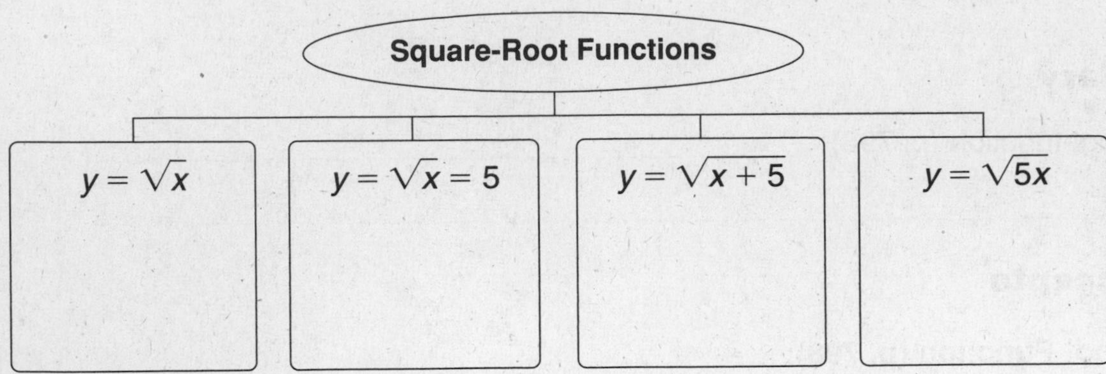

Radical Expressions

Lesson Objectives

Simplify radical expressions

Vocabulary

radical expression (p. 805) ____________________

radicand (p. 805) ____________________

Key Concepts

Simplest Form of a Square-Root Expression (p. 805):

Product Property of Square Roots (p. 806):

WORDS	NUMBERS	ALGEBRA

Quotient Property of Square Roots (p. 806):

WORDS	NUMBERS	ALGEBRA

Think and Discuss (p. 808)

Get Organized

In each box, write the property and give an example.

	Product Property of Square Roots	Quotient Property of Square Roots
Words		
Example		

LESSON 11-7

Adding and Subtracting Radical Expressions

Lesson Objectives

Add and subtract radical expressions

Vocabulary

like radicals (p. 811) ______________________________

____

Key Concepts

Think and Discuss (p. 813)

Get Organized Complete the graphic organizer.

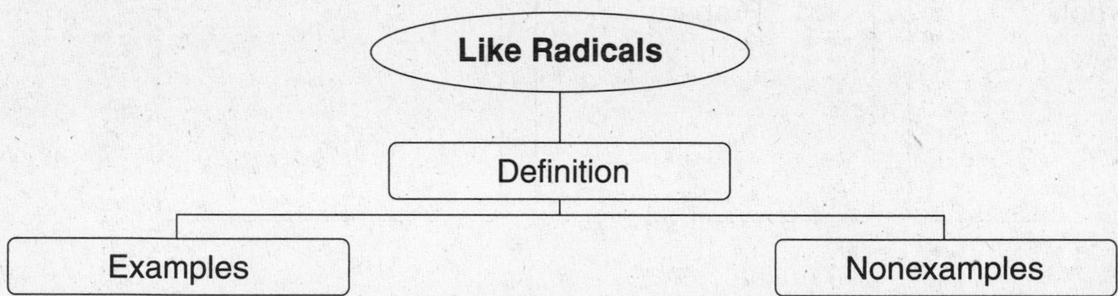

Percents

Lesson Objectives

Multiply and divide radical expression; Rationalize denominators

Key Concepts

Think and Discuss (p. 818)

Get Organized In each box, give an example and show how to simplify it.

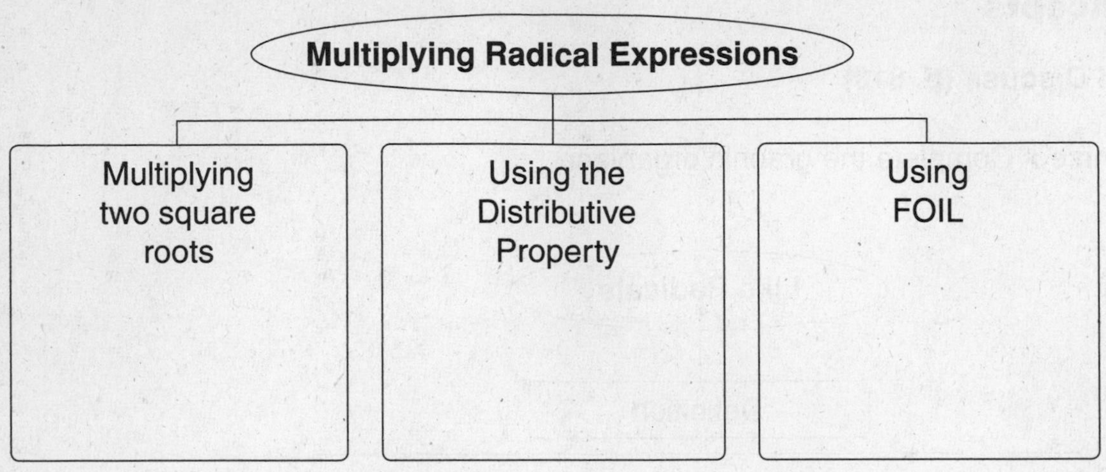

Solving Radical Equations

Lesson Objectives

Solve radical equations

Vocabulary

radical equation (p. 822) ____________________

____

extraneous solution (p. 824) ____________________

____

Key Concepts

Power Property of Equality (p. 822):

WORDS	NUMBERS	ALGEBRA

Think and Discuss (p. 826)

Get Organized Write and solve a radical equation using the boxes to show each step.

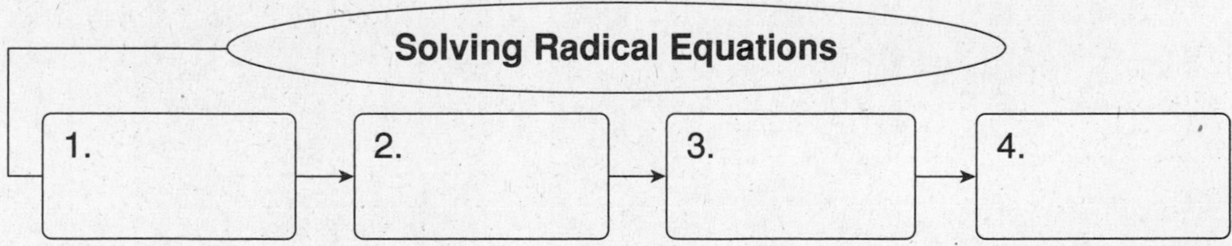

CHAPTER 11

Chapter Review

11-1 Geometric Sequences

Find the next three terms in each geometric sequence.

1. 16, −8, 4, −2, 1, . . . **2.** 0.01, 0.06, 0.36, 2.16, . . . **3.** 1458, 486, 162, 54, . . .

4. What is the 8th term of the geometric sequence 1, 3, 9, 27, . . .?

5. The first term of a geometric sequence is 77, and the common ratio is 0.7. What is the 7th term of the sequence?

6. The ninth term of a geometric sequence is −3. The common ratio is −1. Find the first term of the sequence.

11-2 Exponential Functions

7. The function $f(x) = 2500(0.5)^x$, where x is the time in years, models the number of gaming systems sold to students at a middle school. How many gaming systems will be sold in 4 years?

Graph each exponential function.

8. $y = 6(2)^x$ **9.** $y = -5(0.5)^x$ **10.** $y = -\left(1\frac{1}{2}\right)^x$

11-3 Exponential Growth and Decay

Write a function to model each situation. Then find the value of the function after the given amount of time.

11. Ed invested \$5000 for college tuition and he expects to receive 5% interest annually; 5 years.

12. A \$1600 computer is losing value at a rate of 10% per year; 3 years.

13. \$3500 is invested at a rate of 5.5% compounded quarterly; 4 years.

14. Francium-233 has a half-life of approximately 22 minutes. Find the amount of francium-233 left from an 88-gram sample after 54 minutes.

11-4 Linear, Quadratic, and Exponential Models

Look for a pattern in each data set to determine which kind of model best describes the data.

15. $\{(-20, 17), (-10, 12), (0, 7), (10, 2), (20, -3)\}$

16. $\{(-7, 5), (-6, -4), (-5, -7), (-4, -4), (-3, 5)\}$

Graph each data set. Which kind of model best describes the data?

17. $\{(-2, -12), (2, 2), (6, 8), (10, 6), (14, -4)\}$

18. $\{(-1, 0.125), (0, 0.25), (1, 0.5), (2, 1), (4, 4)\}$

11-5 Square-Root Functions

Find the domain of each square-root function.

19. $y = \sqrt{x + 2} - 1$

20. $y = \sqrt{4x - 1}$

21. $y = \sqrt{2(x - 4) + 3}$

Graph each square-root function.

22. $y = \sqrt{x + 3} - 2$

23. $y = \frac{1}{4}\sqrt{x + 2}$

11-6 Radical Expressions

Simplify. All variables represent nonnegative numbers.

24. $\sqrt{108}$

25. $\sqrt{\frac{324}{4}}$

26. $-\sqrt{25a^4b^6}$

27. $\sqrt{\frac{72}{49}}$

28. $\sqrt{\frac{16a^6}{b^4}}$

29. $\sqrt{\frac{98a^2b^4}{48b^2}}$

30. How long is the diagonal of a football field that is 100 yards long and 50 yards wide? Give the answer as a radical expression in simplest form. Then estimate the length to the nearest yard.

11-7 Adding and Subtracting Radical Expressions

Simplify each expression.

31. $2\sqrt{3} + 5\sqrt{3}$

32. $2\sqrt{7a} + 5\sqrt{63a}$

33. $5\sqrt{3} + 2\sqrt{75}$

34. $4\sqrt{5} + 3\sqrt{7}$

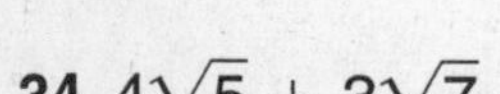

35. $5\sqrt{8} - 3\sqrt{18} + \sqrt{3}$

36. $2\sqrt{20x} + 3\sqrt{5x}$

11-8 Multiplying and Dividing Radical Expressions

Multiply. Write each product in simplest form.

37. $\sqrt{3}\sqrt{5}$

38. $2\sqrt{18}(3\sqrt{8})$

39. $2\sqrt{6}(3\sqrt{7})$

40. $(2\sqrt{5})^2$

41. $(6 - \sqrt{2})(6 + \sqrt{2})$

42. $(\sqrt{a} - 5)(3\sqrt{a} + 7)$

Simplify each quotient.

43. $\frac{\sqrt{6}}{\sqrt{3}}$

44. $\frac{4}{2\sqrt{3}}$

45. $\frac{\sqrt{50}}{\sqrt{y^2}}$

46. $\frac{6\sqrt{10}}{8\sqrt{2}}$

47. $\frac{-12\sqrt{24}}{3\sqrt{2}}$

48. $\frac{2\sqrt{x}}{\sqrt{x} + \sqrt{y}}$

11-9 Solving Radical Equations

Solve each equation. Check your answer.

49. $\sqrt{x} = 5$

50. $\sqrt{2x} - 4 = 2$

51. $\sqrt{x + 7} = 10$

52. $\frac{\sqrt{x}}{4} = 5$

53. $\sqrt{x + 5} - \sqrt{x} = 1$

54. $\sqrt{7 - x} + \sqrt{x + 11} = 6$

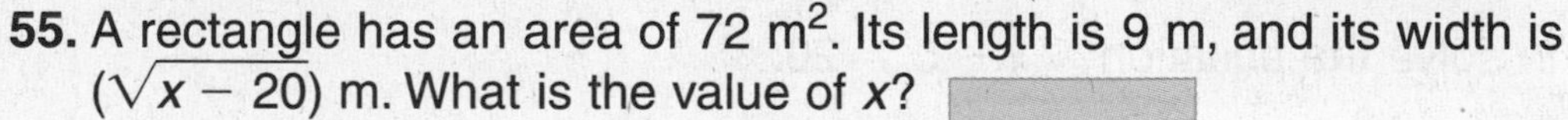

55. A rectangle has an area of 72 m^2. Its length is 9 m, and its width is $(\sqrt{x - 20})$ m. What is the value of x?

CHAPTER 11

Big Ideas

Answer these questions to summarize the important concepts from Chapter 11 in your own words.

1. Explain the difference between exponential growth and exponential decay.

2. When the independent variable changes by a constant amount, what are the characteristics of linear functions, quadratic functions, and exponential functions?

3. Explain the difference between the graphs $f(x) = \sqrt{x} + 4$ and $f(x) = \sqrt{x + 4}$.

4. Explain how you know when a square-root expression is in simplest form.

5. Explain how to solve the equation $\sqrt{x} - 5 = 20$.

For more review of Chapter 11:

- Complete the Chapter 11 Study Guide and Review on pages 836–839 of your textbook.
- Compete the Ready to Go On quizzes on pages 797 and 831 of your textbook.

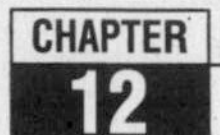

Vocabulary

This table contains important vocabulary terms from Chapter 12. As you work through the chapter, fill in the page number, definition, and a clarifying example for each term.

Term	Page	Definition	Clarifying Example
asymptote			
discontinuous function			
excluded value			
inverse variation			
rational equation			

Term	Page	Definition	Clarifying Example
rational expression			
rational function			

LESSON 12-1

Inverse Variation

Lesson Objectives

Identify, write, and graph inverse variations

Vocabulary

inverse variation (p. 851): ______________________________

____

Key Concepts

Inverse Variations (p. 851):

WORDS	NUMBERS	ALGEBRA

Product Rule for Inverse Variation (p. 853):

Think and Discuss (p. 854)

Get Organized In each box, write an example of the parts of the given inverse variation.

$$y = \frac{8}{x}$$

Constant of variation	Graph	Solutions

LESSON 12-2

Rational Functions

Lesson Objectives

Identify excluded values of rational functions; graph rational functions

Vocabulary

rational function (p. 858): ______________________________

____

excluded value (p. 858): ______________________________

____

discontinuous function (p. 858): ______________________________

____

asymptote (p. 858): ______________________________

____

Key Concepts

Identifying Asymptotes (p. 859):

WORDS	EXAMPLES	

Think and Discuss (p. 862)

Get Organized In each box, find the asymptotes for the given rations function.

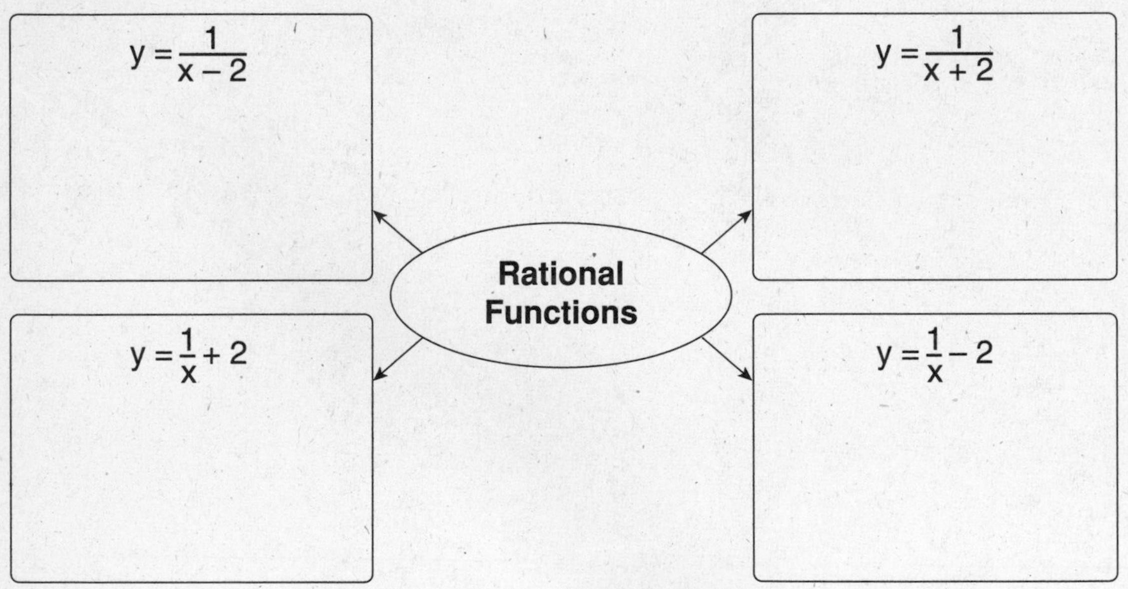

LESSON 12-3

Simplifying Rational Expressions

Lesson Objectives

Simplify rational expressions; Identify excluded values or rational expressions

Vocabulary

rational expression (p. 851): ______________________________

____

Key Concepts

Think and Discuss (p. 869)

Get Organized In each box, find the asymptotes for the given rations function.

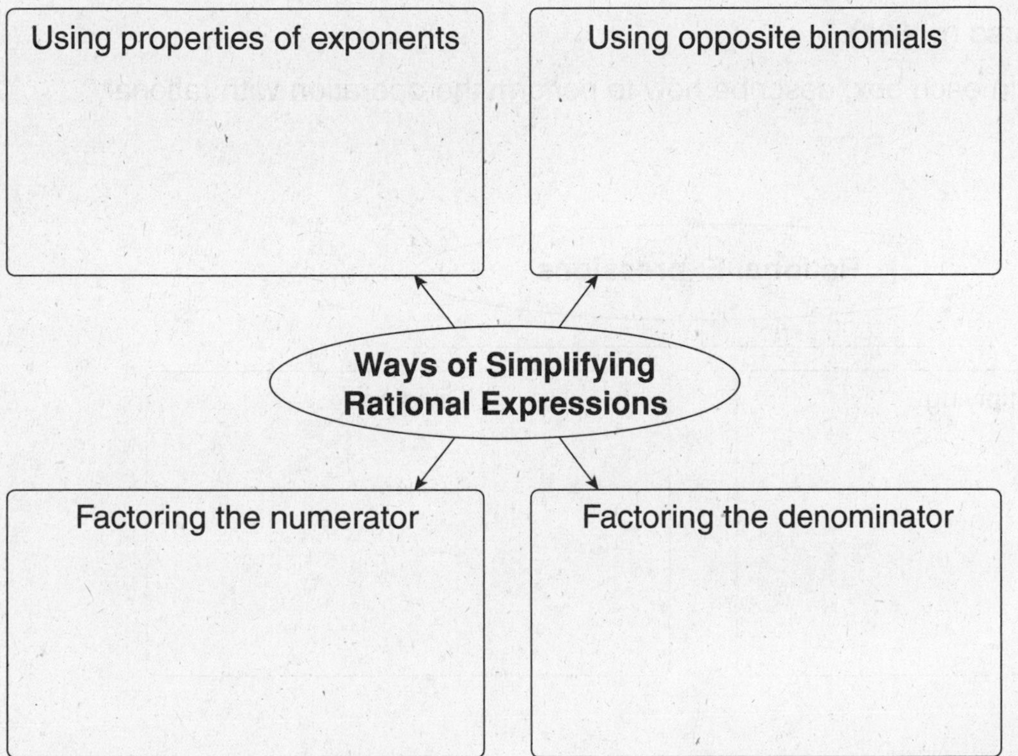

LESSON 12-4

Multiplying and Dividing Rational Expressions

Know it! Note

Lesson Objectives

Multiply and divide rational expressions

Key Concepts

Multiplying Rational Expressions (p. 878):

Dividing Rational Expressions (p. 880):

Think and Discuss (p. 881)

Get Organized In each box, describe how to perform the operation with rational expressions.

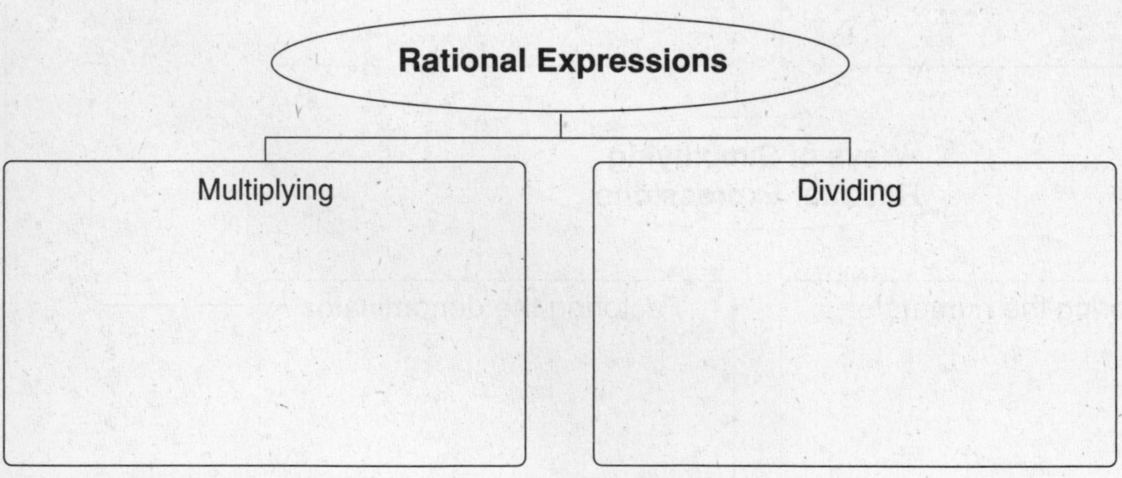

LESSON 12-5

Adding and Subtracting Rational Expressions

Lesson Objectives

add and subtract rational expression with like denominators; add and subtract rational expressions with unlike denominators

Key Concepts

Adding Rational Expressions with Like Denominators (p. 885):

Think and Discuss (p. 888)

Get Organized In each box, compare and contrast operations with fractions and rational numbers.

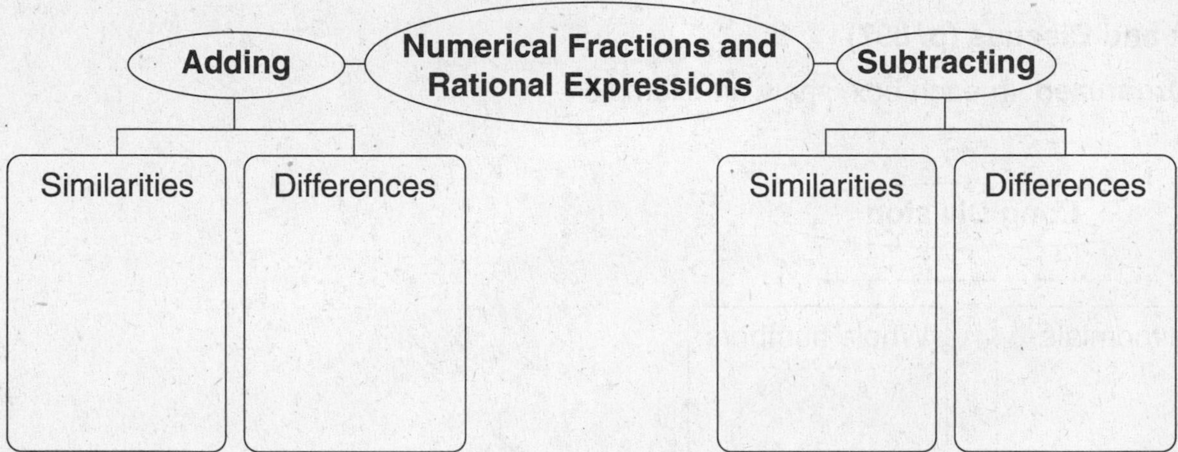

LESSON 12-6

Dividing Polynomials

Lesson Objectives

Divide a polynomial by a monomial or binomial

Key Concepts

Dividing Polynomials (p. 893):

	WORDS	NUMBERS	ALGEBRA
Step 1			
Step 2			
Step 3			

Think and Discuss (p. 897)

Get Organized In each box, show an example

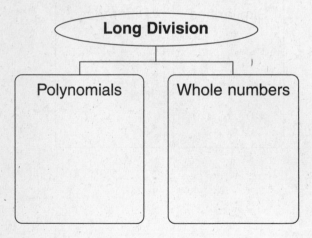

Long Division

Polynomials	Whole numbers

LESSON 12-7

Solving Rational Equations

Lesson Objectives

Solve rational equations; Identify extraneous solutions

Vocabulary

rational equation (p. 900): ______________________________

____

Key Concepts

Think and Discuss (p. 903)

Get Organized In each box, write the solution and check.

Solving Rational Equations

Solve by using cross products.	Solve by using the LCD.

CHAPTER 12

Chapter Review

12-1 Inverse Variation

Tell whether each relationship represents an inverse variation. Explain.

1.

x	−8	−6	−4
y	−2	−3	−4

2. $y = \frac{x}{4}$ 3. $y = \frac{4}{x}$ 4. $xy = -4$ 5. $x + y = -4$

6. Write and graph the inverse variation in which $y = \frac{1}{2}$ and $x = 18$.

12-2 Rational Functions

Identify the excluded values and the vertical and horizontal asymptotes for each rational function. Then graph each function.

7. $y = -\frac{3}{x}$ 8. $y = \frac{5}{x + 3}$ 9. $y = \frac{5}{2x - 10} + 1$

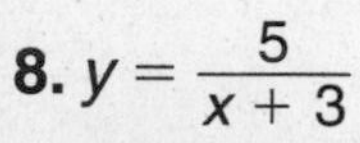

12-3 Simplifying Rational Expressions

Simplify each rational expression, if possible. Identify any excluded values.

10. $\frac{8x^4}{2x^5}$

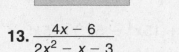

11. $\frac{12x - 6}{14x - 7}$

12. $\frac{8 - x}{x^2 - 7x - 8}$

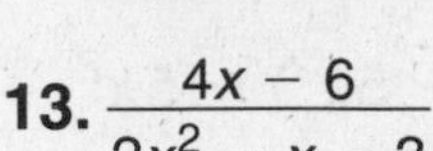

13. $\frac{4x - 6}{2x^2 - x - 3}$

14. $\frac{x^2 + 4x}{x^2 - 16}$

15. $\frac{4x^2 + 3x - 10}{25 - 16x^2}$

12-4 Multiplying and Dividing Rational Expressions

Multiply or divide. Simplify your answer.

16. $\frac{7x^2}{3} \cdot \frac{9}{14x}$

17. $\frac{9x^2}{x^2 + 12x + 36} \div \frac{12x}{x^2 + 6x}$

18. $\frac{x^2 + 2x - 15}{x^2 - 4x - 45} \div \frac{x^2 + x - 12}{x^2 - 5x - 36}$

19. $\frac{25x^2 - 20x + 4}{x^2 - 1} \cdot \frac{x + 1}{10x - 4}$

12-5 Adding and Subtracting Rational Expressions

Add or subtract. Simplify your answer.

20. $\frac{y^2}{y - 1} - \frac{1}{y - 1}$

21. $\frac{10x}{5x - 2} + \frac{7x - 2}{5x - 2}$

22. $\frac{8}{y^2 - 4y} + \frac{2}{y}$

23. $\dfrac{x}{x^2 + x - 2} - \dfrac{1}{x + 2}$

24. $\dfrac{x}{x^2 - 5x + 6} - \dfrac{3}{x - 3}$

25. $\dfrac{1}{x + y} + \dfrac{3x - 3y}{x^2 - y^2}$

12-6 Dividing Polynomials

Divide.

26. $(21x^3 - 35x^2) \div 7x$

27. $(8x^4 - 3x^3) \div x^2$

28. $(25x^5 + 15x^4 - 5x^2) \div 5x^2$

Divide using long division.

29. $(x^2 + 9x + 14) \div (x + 7)$

30. $(x^2 - 9x - 10) \div (x + 1)$

31. $(3x^3 - 5x^2 + 10x - 3) \div 3x + 1$

12-7 Solving Rational Equations

Solve. Check your answers.

32. $\dfrac{x - 1}{15} = \dfrac{2}{5}$

33. $x + 1 = \dfrac{72}{x}$

34. $\dfrac{10}{x(x - 2)} + \dfrac{4}{x} = \dfrac{5}{x - 2}$

30. Don can stock shelves in 5 hours. It takes Kim 3 hours to stock the same shelves. How long will it take them to stock the shelves if they work together?

CHAPTER 12

Big Ideas

Answer these questions to summarize the important concepts from Chapter 12 in your own words.

1. Explain why $y = \frac{1}{x-3}$ has an asymptote at $x = 3$.

2. When is a rational expression in simplest form?

3. What are the steps for adding or subtracting rational expressions?

4. What are the steps for using long division to divide a polynomial by a binomial?

For more review of Chapter 12:

- Complete the Chapter 12 Study Guide and Review on pages 910–913 of your textbook.
- Compete the Ready to Go On quizzes on pages 877 and 907 of your textbook.